Tin Can Man

Tin Can Man

E. J. Jernigan

NAVAL INSTITUTE PRESS
Annapolis, Maryland

This book has been brought to publication with the generous assistance of Marguerite and Gerry Lenfest.

Naval Institute Press
291 Wood Road
Annapolis, MD 21402

First Naval Institute Press paperback edition published 2010.

Library of Congress Cataloging-in-Publication Data

Jernigan, E. J. (Emory J.), 1923–
Tin can man / Emory J. Jernigan.—1st Naval Institute Press pbk. ed.
    p. cm.
Originally published: Arlington, VA: Vandemere Press, 1993.
Includes index.
ISBN 978-1-59114-424-3 (alk. paper)
1. Jernigan, E. J. (Emory J.), 1923– 2. Saufley (Destroyer) 3. World War, 1939–1945—Campaigns—Pacific Area. 4. World War, 1939–1945—Naval operations, American. 5. World War, 1939–1945—Personal narratives, American. 6. United States. Navy—Biography. 7. Sailors—United States—Biography. I. Title.

D774.S316J47 2008
940.54'5973092—dc22

                            2007037186

Printed in the United States of America on acid-free paper

16 15 14 13 12 11 10   9 8 7 6 5 4 3 2
First printing

To my wife, Ann Rivenbark Jernigan,
I love her then, now and forever!

ACKNOWLEDGEMENT

To Karen and Bill Comer, you will never know the depth of my love. Thanks!

To Captain Richard E. Pearsall, U.S.N. (Ret.), who would have enjoyed our war! Thanks for your help with "Tin Can Man" and the bell.

Thanks to my shipmates, all of you!

To Bill and Sandy Robbins and kids, you gave me hope at all times.

To my two sons, Mike and Cy, and my daughter, Karen, you have helped on my bad days after Momma left and gave me good advice when I needed you.

To Willis Martin Norman, the man who furnished friendship and devotion over the years, supplied all of our machine shop entertainment, and who, along with O. R. Elliott, furnished the pictures of the ship and shipmates.

And most of all, I love you, Bob and Laura Cromie. Thanks for your help with Ann.

Fritz Heinzen, who encouraged me and found my friend and publisher, Art Brown.

Admiral Bert F. Brown, who pushed me to do the book.

Dr. L. L. Simms, thanks for your help and advice.

And all my friends in every state of our great and wonderful country.

My special thanks to that nice lady with all the red ink who pushed, pulled and bullied me as she made my book flow better and learned about talleywhackers, ding-dongs, and bubbles. Pat Burger, I love you also.

TABLE OF CONTENTS

| CHAPTER ONE | **THE ITCH TO GO**
 JANUARY 1940 – MARCH 1941 | 13 |

| CHAPTER TWO | **A BOOT IN THE USS WASHINGTON**
 MARCH 1941 – DECEMBER 1941 | 31 |

CHAPTER ONE — **THE ITCH TO GO** — JANUARY 1940 – MARCH 1941 — 13

CHAPTER TWO — **A BOOT IN THE USS WASHINGTON** — MARCH 1941 – DECEMBER 1941 — 31

CHAPTER THREE — **SHOCK AT DAWN** — DECEMBER 1941 – SEPTEMBER 1942 — 54

CHAPTER FOUR — **DESTROYER DUTY** — SEPTEMBER 1942 – DECEMBER 1942 — 77

CHAPTER FIVE — **UNDER THE SOUTHERN CROSS** — DECEMBER 1942 – MARCH 1943 — 94

CHAPTER SIX — **DEATH AND THE FLUTTER-WILLIES (and Remember These Things)** — MARCH 1943 – JULY 1943 — 105

CHAPTER SEVEN — **IN THE LAND DOWN UNDER** — JULY 1943 – AUGUST 1943 — 127

CHAPTER EIGHT — **HELL UNLEASHED** — AUGUST 1943 – DECEMBER 1943 — 138

CHAPTER NINE — **WE ALL HAD A THOUSAND YARD STARE** — DECEMBER 1943 – AUGUST 1944 — 146

CHAPTER TEN — **UNDER THE BAY BRIDGE** — AUGUST 1944 – NOVEMBER 1944 — 163

CHAPTER ELEVEN — **RISING SUN SETTING** — NOVEMBER 1944 – NOVEMBER 1945 — 174

EPILOGUE — 195

INDEX — 199

Tin Can Man

⚓ 1 ⚓

THE ITCH TO GO

JANUARY 1940 – MARCH 1941

I was born in Chattahoochee, Florida, on September 20, 1923, to Emory Jernigan and Mattie Ferrell Jernigan. We moved to Grandma's farm to take care of her, an event I can't remember. Two brothers and two sisters were born to us at the farm: Naomi, Thomas, Mattie Lee, and James. Our garden assured us of plenty to eat even though we had no money, no electricity, and no car. Mule and wagon transportation was a must. We walked a lot and, to us, five miles was no more than a walk around the block today. When tools wore out or farm equipment broke, there was no money to repair it. Broken bones went unset many times. I saw some old people who had bones that never mended. Prime land was sold for $1.00 an acre by the county and state government to pay taxes that were owed. Proud people had to ask for help. President Hoover handed out food and clothes marked, "Not to be sold." It broke men's hearts to take these things. All they wanted to do was work for a living. A depression kills the soul of all men.

The women lived in a different world. Their outlook was barefoot, pregnant, and over the washpot in the backyard. Thank God for the moms of that day. They were the best people I have ever known. Franklin D. Roosevelt became President on March 4, 1933, and started the work programs. The Works Projects Administration's Civilian Conservation Corps

13

camps were set up in a paramilitary form to put young men to work.

My goal in those youthful days was to enter the military. I preferred the Marines and would go see a Marine recruiter every time one was in our area. They would always laugh and say to come back when I was older. I never considered the Navy. There was a Navy base of sorts in Jacksonville with a few sailors, lots of Army, and a few Marines. The old-timers said that the Army did the work, the Marines got the credit, and the Navy got the pay. I wanted action, money, and glamour, seeing myself as a hero if we ever got into a war during my lifetime. It was like sitting outside a big restaurant and smelling food when you were hungry and broke. I wanted to get in the Marine Corps very much in those days. I never made it.

I kept getting more and more frustrated with these rejections until finally I threatened to go to Canada and volunteer to fight in their military forces. Mom and Dad decided I could join the Civilian Conservation Corps which was like the military and might satisfy me. So I signed up and headed off for Camp 1410 in Cross City, Florida, not knowing that I was starting a journey that would take nearly five years before my return home to live among the people I loved. I was just happy to get away at the time.

Glen W. Martin was the camp commander; Dr. Wexelblatt was the doctor at the camp. A noncommissioned officer named Carbarea was in charge of recruits. We worked hard on roads, dams, and parks, which are part of our heritage today. The food was good, and we fattened up and grew stronger each day. On long weekends I would go with some of the boys to Jacksonville, Orlando, or Tampa. What fun we had! My total pay was $35.00 a month. I had been given a $5.00 raise because I was an assistant first-aid man in addition to my regular job duties. Each month I sent $15.00 home and kept the rest for myself. I was enjoying the life, but I still wanted to get into one of the military services in the worst way.

In September 1940, a Navy recruiting officer came to sign people up at the camp. He was Chief Yeoman C. E. Ely with many years in service. The stripes on his arm and his rating were in gold, which meant he had been a *good boy* for a long time. I thought that his uniform was the prettiest I had ever seen. A sailor with him had on a white uniform with red stripes. I thought it was right pretty but the gold was best. I could see myself in a uniform like that in all the great ports of the world: New York City, San Francisco, London, and all the exotic places of the Far East where the most beautiful girls swarmed around only to have their hearts broken when I sailed away. With dreams of this kind, I got in line. When the chief talked to me, I told him I was only 16 years old. He said, "We'll be starting the new kiddy cruises sometime in December. I can come back for you then." (A kiddy cruise meant you were in the Navy from age 17 to 21; then you were discharged.)

I made every preparation to enlist. First, I went back home for Mom and Dad to sign the papers. I gave different people for references regarding my character as I prepared to get into the service. In my exuberance I figured I would be dressed up like the chief in no time at all. Of course, you had to be a good boy to get all those gold stripes, and I stood about as much chance of doing that as a mouse had in a cathouse. I was sad when I realized that I couldn't get those stripes right away.

Of the 21 of us trying to get in the Navy that day, 3 made it. We were sent by train from Jacksonville, Florida, to Macon, Georgia. On December 2, 1940, Lt. W. R. Johnson, USN, gave us a little speech that impressed me greatly and then swore us in. I think every one of us was ready to explode with joy. We were in the Navy!

At the swearing-in, I was standing in the back row of recruits near five steps. In my excitement, I didn't notice the brush and can of floor polish indicating the recently polished condition of the floor. As I turned to go, I slipped and fell hitting my left knee on all five steps and ending at the bottom with my knee and pride hurt. The doctor gave me a cursory exam, wrote it in my record, and sent me on my way.

Up to that point, Macon was the greatest distance I had

been from home. Now I was headed on a train for the Naval Operating Base in Norfolk, Virginia, and I was as excited as a new bride. We saw people everywhere and always stared at Navy officers. We had meals in the dining car. The countryside flew by. I counted telegraph poles as they flashed by, lost count, and started over. The world outside the window was composed of farms, cattle, and barns with advertisements of all kinds painted on them. Burma Shave signs on parallel roads sped by faster than I could read them. It was a new and wondrous way to live. On top of everything else, I was drawing $21.00 a month for all this fun! There was only one thing I needed now: girls! girls! girls! They were everywhere, dressed in fine clothes, blushing when our eyes met and then looking the other way. I felt like a spring bee in the first flower petal of the year.

My first impression of Norfolk, Virginia, was how dirty it was. Coming in on the railroad, we could see old newspapers and trash against the fences and in the street gutters. Rundown buildings had sleepy looking people, both men and women, in the doorways sitting or lying around with empty bottles everywhere.

I can still remember the smell going through Norfolk and out to the Navy base. A young man like myself out of the backwoods wasn't used to the smell of warehouses, stored fruit, and exhaust fumes. We arrived at the Naval Operating Base at night. We were assigned to a building and bunk. When we went in and turned on the lights, roaches went scampering every which way. That didn't stop us from going to bed as we were tired from riding on the train. The knee that I had hurt in Macon was bothering me pretty bad.

The Naval Base had barracks from World War I. The most impressive thing about the base was the fence around it. They had you fenced in and other people fenced out. At the top of the fence were strings of barbed wire to keep a man in or out. The base was big and sprawling with clean grounds and drill fields. The wooden buildings were gleaming white with fresh paint. The old brick buildings had cleaned brick walls, new caulking everywhere, and brightly polished floors. The piers had old four-piper destroyers and two aircraft carriers tied up to them. One of the aircraft carriers was the USS *Ranger*.

I was placed in a platoon ruled over by Chief Turret Captain Mettick, who was back from retirement into a Navy that no longer carried his rating. He was a Chief Turret Captain, permanent appointment, USN, and he let us know it in no uncertain way. He told us we were too damn dumb to stay on the farm, let alone become sailors.

One of the first things we had to learn was Navy time. Our Navy watches for sailing and standing watch are shown below:

Civilian Time	Navy Time
The midwatch (midnight to 4:00 AM)	0000 to 0400
The morning watch (4:00 AM to 8:00 AM)	0400 to 0800
The forenoon watch (8:00 AM to noon)	0800 to 1200
The afternoon watch (noon to 4:00 PM)	1200 to 1600
The dog watch (4:00 PM to 8:00 PM)	1600 to 2000
The first watch (8:00 PM to midnight)	2000 to 2400

Navy time runs from midnight 0000 hours to 2400 (the following midnight). Thus, as civilian time goes, you count 0000 to 1200 for the morning hours and 1200 to 2400 for the second half of the day. While I was in the Navy, I did it the Navy way. In my book, I've done it my way!

They woke us up about 4:00 AM and double-timed us to the chow hall for breakfast. We had baked beans. I had never heard of such an outrageous thing as beans for breakfast. They served them twice a week throughout the Navy. They were great after you had eaten them for a while. The first day, I had a couple of donuts that always went with the Navy beans, but didn't touch the beans. Had I known what kind of day they had in store for us, I would have eaten every last bean. They lined us up again and gave us all kinds of shots. Then, naked, we were examined by the doctor and a pharmacist's mate who checked us for venereal disease. It was, "Pull it back, milk it down." If you didn't do it right, the pharmacist's mate would grab you and jerk it half off. He did this to get your attention. It was extremely effective.

Next, we moved on to where they issued uniforms. I had never been fitted out in such a hurry in my life. My hat was too little; my pants hung way down on me. My clothes were either too big or too small. Everyone either hated or loved the white hats issued to us for dress and work uniforms. The hat was supposed to be worn rounded off two inches above the eyes, very tilted fore and aft, so that even a light stern breeze would dislodge it. Mine blew off many times on city streets and at sea. Each sailor had his own way of trying to look good in one of these hats so they wound up being worn as many different ways as there were sailors. I had a love/hate feeling for mine and still do.

The neckerchief had the same function in Navy life as a tie did in civilian life. It was folded into a triangle, rolled and tucked under the jumper collar, and tied in the front. It looked good and served us well.

Jumpers were tight-fitting and looked best when they were so tight you needed help in putting them on. Pulling them over your head was like skinning a squirrel. Our bell-bottom trousers were worn tight and buttoned with two buttons at the front with a flap that had thirteen buttons and was as big as the opening in a coal chute. When you had to get to your talleywhacker, you unbuttoned a vertical row of buttons right and left and a horizontal row at the top, dropped the flap, and you could water the garden.

Our peacoats were very warm and almost waterproof. I was never cold in one. We had a flat hat for dress blue uniforms with a band imprinted with the ship or station on which you served. They were a good-looking addition to the uniform. Watch caps or peacaps, like the peacoats, were warm for those cold, windy, rainy watches at sea. I loved the enlisted men's uniform just as it was and hoped it would never change.

Our shoes were not fitted to our feet; they were just sized and thrown at us. Mine were black low-cut shoes, the best I had ever had; but I could move my foot an inch fore and aft in the shoe and side to side an inch or more. I wore them over to Chief Mettick. He had me return them to supply with a note.

Before the supply clerk had finished, Chief Mettick came in and looked at my shoes. He then looked at me, shook his head, and asked if I had ever worn shoes before. They fit and didn't blister my feet like the shoes of many of my shipmates. It's hard to believe Chief Mettick helped me!

Supply issued us all our clothes, including a seabag shaped like a long bucket and made of canvas tied with a drawstring at the top. Of course, we didn't know anything at all about how our clothes should be packed. Nothing could be hung or stored on the bunks. The first big test was to get all those clothes into the seabag. We had to roll our white pants up and keep them on the seam so they would stay pressed; we rolled our blues and jumpers and tied them with a string at each end and in the middle. Packing everything into that seabag was like trying to put a ten-pound kitty in a two-pound box. All this time, Chief Mettick was stomping around through the barracks room. He'd grab one man's jumper, stomp on it, and tell him, "Roll the damn thing right or give your heart to God and your ass to me." Then he'd come to the next recruit and raise hell with him about his shoes. Every once in a while, he'd skip by someone who would think how lucky he was! When he got to me, he tore everything up. I didn't have one thing correct. Thompson, the guy beside me, had been in the Army and everything he did was right. He became our platoon leader. I never saw him again after boot camp, and I don't know what happened to him. He sure helped me a lot in the next few weeks at the base.

The most humiliating thing was when they marched us to the barbershop. Men came out with their ears sticking out of their shiny skulls and yelled, "You'll be sorry! You'll be sorry." Older sailors would go by yelling, "Fresh meat! Fresh meat!" The barber was the most sadistic man I've seen in my whole life. You sat in the chair and he clipped you like a sheep. When your hair hit the deck, you were a first class boot. It was the best way I could think of to break a man into the hard job he had to do. Everyone even looked alike.

After enduring several hours of Chief Mettick's raising all

kinds of hell with us in the morning, he told us he'd let us have our afternoon meal even though we didn't deserve it. We had to fall out on the double and double-time it to the chow hall. The line wound all over the place. We went to the back and waited for what seemed an eternity before it was finally our turn to eat. Everyone was nervous and beginning to worry about whether the chief was really going to kill us.

The Navy served us good food, yet many of my shipmates griped about it constantly. The food was strange to me. For breakfast, we had chipped beef and gravy on toast, French toast, scrambled eggs and hash browns (which I had never had), baked beans, doughnuts, boneless ham, Swift's sausage, and bacon. At home, we had grown, killed, and cured all the red meat we ate. Navy food had a much different taste; it was more seasoned and tasted a lot better to me. They served no grits, which I really missed. We had beef for lunch and dinner with fresh vegetables, corn bread, rolls, cake, and milk as well as coffee. Pork chops, liver, chicken, fruits of all kinds, and cereal also appeared frequently. In spite of all the griping, we consumed much food and I think everyone loved it.

Back at the barracks, Chief Mettick introduced us to a big bar of the saltwater soap made by the Octogen Soap Company and a brush used to scrub Navy decks. He found some poor sucker, claimed his neck was dirty, and got a working party of three men to take that poor boy to the head and scrub his body. The chief said, "Everyone better be clean in my platoon from now on or, by God, we'll use all the saltwater soap the Navy's got in Norfolk." They really put you through the physical grinder when you arrived at the base. I was in good condition, which helped. Some of the men had never worked or been free to roam the woods and streams; they had a hard time adjusting to Navy life. One of the men in our group recognized a boatswain mate second class from his hometown. When they talked, the recruit whined about our reception. The boatswain very abruptly told him, "Quit bitching—you weren't drafted," and walked away.

Waking up in the barracks was a shock. Chief Mettick or

the Master-at-Arms would come in, turn on all the lights, beat on the steel bunks with a club, and yell, "Off your ass and on your feet." There was hell to pay if you weren't up the second time they came through!

The chief started trying to teach us a bed was a bunk; upstairs was topside; the rifle was what you shot the enemy with; a gun was what you shot girls with. Anyone behind you was astern; to the right was starboard; to the left was port. The bath was the head; you drank water from a scuttlebutt. The window was a porthole. To work was called turning to; the kitchen was a galley; a light was a lantern; a light on a ship was a running light. We had to learn all of these things immediately. In addition, we had a book called, *The Blue Jacket's Manual*. It was our Bible.

Chief Mettick also taught us to tie knots. I was lucky and knew how to tie all the knots, and I could even splice a rope; for once, I got to help others with knot-tying. He even patted me on my shoulder and said, "Well done." I wanted to knock him down and give him the boot!

The rifle was our reason to exist. We had to keep it cleaned and shined. Our rifles were all old bolt-action weapons from World War I. I had learned to shoot a different way and could hit a squirrel easily in top of a tree. Their way, I was barely able to pass the shooting test. We also learned to stack rifles. To prove our skills, we stacked and restacked them until they were almost worn out. We exercised with the rifles until our arms were dead tired. We did pushups, jumping jacks, situps, and squat-and-walk or duck waddle. If the chief didn't like what we were doing, sometimes he'd almost lift us off of the ground with a big old saber he carried strapped on him. You didn't dare hit him back, but I wanted to lots of times. He seemed to take a perverse happiness in hitting me in the butt. We ran double-time everywhere we went; it was the rule of the day. We also had to swim or learn to swim. I passed this test easily.

We had to learn to row and were placed in groups to report to the ugliest, meanest seaman in the Navy with three hash marks on his sleeve. We could see where his first class rate had been stripped away. He looked wrinkled and mean, and he worked us until our backs hurt and our hands blistered. After two lessons, we could row round and round in the bay, making no headway at all. I dug the paddle too deep and messed everyone up. When I dug too shallow, I fell back on the man behind me. Everyone kept falling back on the man astern of them. The seaman raised hell with us, made us ship oars, and said we might have to walk ashore. Cussing us as a group, he steered for the dock to tell Chief Mettick he was through with us (and we were glad).

We had two things issued to us together with our shoes and clothes. They were most important to Chief Mettick. One was a sewing kit and the other was a little ditty bag with a shoebrush and polish. He expected our shoes to be polished to perfection. He would run you all day long and inspect your shoes that afternoon. When he was dismissing you, the shoes better look just as sharp as when you went out. Even if the shoes were good, he'd find some reason to raise hell with you. This cantankerous old man was out to get us individually and collectively; and what a job he was doing!

Down at the chow hall and in the brief intermission periods we had, we'd get to talk with people in other platoons. According to them, their platoon leaders were meaner than ours. When two or three of the chiefs got together, we thought they were plotting against us. Even when they laughed, we worried. When they picked one of us to make an example, that was hell day. All of us had to wash our own clothes and hang them to dry. We kept our clothes rolled on the seam and tied tightly with string, much in the shape of rolled-up newspaper. It was the only way to store our clothes since we had no lockers. Clothes brushes kept lint off the wool jumpers, pants, and peacoats. Our shoes were spit-shined. What little beard we had was shaved so closely that our faces were sore in cold weather.

After many weeks went by, we were looking pretty sharp on the drill field. I thought that was the best thing we did. I was even starting to like Chief Mettick.

On Christmas Eve, Chief Mettick promoted me to "Captain of the Head" from noon to 4:00 PM. I could have boiled him in oil! At 4:00 PM, I joined the other boots singing Christmas carols and acting happy until midnight. All of us were as homesick as we could be. I think everyone dropped a few tears on Navy pillows that night. I would have done anything for a hug from Mom. We were getting harsh treatment and pretty rough talk. We were all learning to be warriors, which was what it was all about, and Chief Mettick was in his glory.

On that Christmas Day, we slept until noon and turkey time. Everyone was sad, happy, and lonely at the same time and thankful when the Navy routine started anew. That December 25, 1940, was to be our last peaceful Christmas until 1945.

One day, one of the senior officers came out as we marched by. He called Chief Mettick over and gave him a well-done comment for the platoon. The chief walked back out and drilled us hard for another few minutes, took us to the barracks, and dismissed us. He came in a few minutes later and made us clean the decks. When I happened to call it the floor, he got in front of me with his fists balled up, his face red, and told me I was stupid for not calling it a deck. He said I'd better remember that fact for as long as I was in the Navy, maybe as long as I lived because I might not live to get out of the Navy. I was learning that you better do and say things the Navy way.

The next day, with a week left in training, I was on the drill field in an inside column. Chief Mettick said, "March right." I marched left and tied up the whole platoon worse than an accident on a California freeway. When he dismissed the platoon, he kept me. For punishment, I had to refill a bucket of water hanging on the stacking swivel of my rifle several times as he double-timed me around the indoor hanger where we trained in inclement weather. I ran until I got as cold and wet as the proverbial well-digger's ass. The next day I was in sick bay with *catfever*, a form of the flu. I didn't even get to see my platoon graduate. Instead I was introduced to Navy needles and pharmacist's mates. Chief Turret Captain Mettick, permanent appointment, USN (retired), came to see me in sick bay and gruffly informed me that if I didn't learn my right from my left, I'd probably spend the rest of my kiddy cruise in boot camp. I'll swear that I saw a tear on each cheek as he turned to leave. I learned to listen to instructions from this experience. Later, when I ran across Chief Mettick, he treated me as if nothing had happened.

Because of my illness, I was assigned to another platoon commanded by Chief Duvall. He and Chief Mettick were cut from the same cloth. Mettick's face had been round and happy-looking although he was never happy. Duvall's face was all wrinkled. It looked like he had been to sea all his life and the saltwater had made a prune out of it. He was a small man. The first thing he did was get right up in my face and tell me I must really be a stupid person to have been sent back here to screw up his platoon. I got a good start with him; he disliked me to begin with. I was his daily whipping boy for three weeks until my training was finished.

All things have an end, and I was finally through with boot camp. When a young man finished with Mettick and Duvall and left for the expanding two-ocean Navy, he was ready to become part of the cutting edge of the greatest Navy ever to sail on any sea. Bleeding hearts cried about how they treated people in boot camp and at Parris Island, and even in the Army training camps. There was one thing you had to do at these camps in the short time you were a recruit; you had to learn to obey any order, no matter how trivial, to be on a winning team. It was that simple. One man could disobey and end up costing a battle or sinking a ship. The officers, chiefs, and petty officers did a good job. They taught us to listen. It was not unusual to see a whole platoon of men sweeping a sidewalk with tooth-brushes, running around the drill hall, doing pushups, or getting hit in the butt with a saber. These officers did anything to make you miserable and break your spirit so that you would not fail to do as you were told. It was one of the requirements of the military service that is a success. The only thing they wanted you to learn in boot camp was to obey, keep your clothes

Duval's salty recruits. Graduating Platoon 192. Naval Training School, Norfolk, VA. January 1941. Author is second from left, top row.

OFFICIAL U.S. NAVY PHOTO

clean, look neat, think good thoughts about the service, and build self-respect. You learned to obey no matter what happened.

When graduation day came, we had worked a week or more on marching in formation and how to pass the reviewing stand. We dressed and checked each other with critical eyes, looking for a hair out of place or a spot of dirt. Shoes were like mirrors, spit-shined again and again. Polish was rubbed in by hand, and then a match was struck and held near the shoe. Aqua Velva was spread over the shoes and they were polished some more. Leggings were relaced and rifles checked once more as we listened to Chief Duvall warn us about screwing up. The captain of the base was in the reviewing stand with many flag-rank officers, their wives, and kids. Everyone was dressed fit to kill. Some of the parents of members of our platoon also came. We marched by in perfect order and wondered why we couldn't march by again. When Chief Duvall dismissed us, we tossed our hats in the air, hugged one another, and gathered around the chief who was by then emotional. He told us we would make the best sailors on earth! Some of us went to the barbershop and yelled at the new boots, "You'll be sorry . . . you'll be sorry . . . fresh meat . . . fresh meat!" I stored Chiefs Mettick and Duvall in my memories in the love/hate section where they are alive to this day.

When we finished boot camp, I came down with the mumps. My jaw was swollen and one of my testicles was hurting. I thought I was going to die. They sent me to the Portsmouth Naval Hospital and the rest of the platoon went home on leave. All my belongings were stored, so all I took to the hospital was a ditty bag containing a toothbrush, soap, razor, sewing materials, and a few other things. We had gowns that were too short, too little, and exposed too much. I was embarrassed, to say the least. It was my first time in a hospital and I was scared out of my wits. Men in the platoon had told me I wouldn't be able to have children, maybe not even have sex, after the mumps. A doctor and nurse came in to look at my ding-a-ling which almost pushed me off my rocker. This was a woman looking at a man in front of all the people on the ward.

I had no more than landed in the hospital when another nurse walked in. Her name was Doris Broom and she was a lieutenant from my hometown. Ten years older than I was, she had seen my name on the roster. I could not have been any happier to see anyone. She talked to me and assured me that I'd get well soon, go home for a reunion, and then join the fleet and be happy ever after.

When I recovered they let me have 15 days of leave. I drew $15.00, which was all they would give me so I would have money when I returned. Our total pay was $21.00 dollars per month. They furnished our initial uniforms free, but we had to buy our own after that.

When I reached Chattahoochee, there wasn't a soul there to meet me at the station. Far from seeing me as a hero, Chattahoochee didn't even notice I had come home. I couldn't catch a ride out to the house and had to walk about five miles. When I got home, there wasn't anyone there to meet me. It was a homecoming without anything happening. I'll never forget how disappointed I was. My little brothers and sisters said, "Oh, you look thinner than you did when you left. Your hair's too short." The girls didn't take to the uniform like I thought they would. I had a bad 15 days and went back to Norfolk.

When I arrived in Norfolk, all the people who had been in either platoon with me were gone to faraway places and I was all by myself at the base. For a while I got to see downtown Norfolk and Portsmouth. Norfolk was the biggest place I had ever seen. It was a great port city that had never grown up. Norfolk had a fine naval base, with first-rate shipyards, and excellent repair facilities, but access to the surrounding localities was very limited. Ferryboats were used where they now have bridges and tunnels.

At that time, I met a sailor in the barracks. We went ashore, caught a taxi to Norfolk with several other sailors, and got out at the Shamrock Beer Garden. It was big enough to plant corn in and lined from one end to the other with sailors sipping suds. The tables were full of gobs, girls, and big pitchers of beer. The noise level hurt your ears as the jukebox played *Walking the Floor Over You*, competing with sounds of conversations. As 17-year-olds, we couldn't buy beer, so we went walking. We strolled through a big archway to Arch Street, returned, and went to an old house at 1000 E. Main Street where we stood and watched old salts, seamen first class, and various petty officers ring a bell at a thick wooden door. A bouncer answered the door and let them in while a steady stream of sailors departed. It was payday and fun time. We shook our heads at one another and caught a ferry to Newport News. We rode the same ferry back and returned to base where the Marine on guard duty gave our morale a big boost. He patted us down to see if we had any whiskey hidden in our clothes. (Damn, we were brave!)

Beer gardens in Norfolk were easier to find than a traffic light. When payday for the fleet came, it was standing room only. Once I went to a beer joint called the Arab's Tent with a ship's cook from the base. He was older and could buy beer. He slipped some to me. As the beer had its effect, he kept bumping my knee with his and later put his hand on my leg. I jerked my leg away and he quit. When I went to the head, he followed. As I was buttoning my bellbottoms, he grabbed my talleywhacker, which scared hell out of me. I blocked him into the bulkhead so hard he crumpled to the deck and I hauled ass! Minus a hat and scared of being picked up for being out of uniform, I was walking faster than a horse could trot when a taxi pulled up with three sailors going back to the base. At the gate, the Marine on guard duty wanted to know where my hat was and laughed when I told him. I was humiliated in front of everyone, walked fast to my quarters, and hit my sack!

Most of the people seemed to work directly or indirectly for the Navy or Naval support facilities. Another group worked in goods and services. Tailors made fine dress blues, which enlisted men were not supposed to have but everyone did. Tatoo artists would decorate your body and they were very good at it. I have seen old sailors covered in tatoos from their chest down to their waist and many below their waist. Some had X-rated pictures; others had beautiful pictures, like a mural of the sea. The very best tatoos were on those who had served in the Asiatic fleet where the Michelangelos of the tatoo artists plied their trade.

At the end of boot training, Chief Duvall had called us all together for sex education. He said, "The girls in Norfolk can give you more grief in ten minutes than the Navy can in four years." He held a rubber aloft and said, "Use this and then check in at a pro station set up for the prevention of sexual disease. They are open all night. The pharmacist's mate will show you what to do. If you catch VD, the Navy will put you on restriction and stop your pay until you are cured. You will make up the time at the end of your cruise." Much of our anticipation evaporated after that little speech.

The girls who followed the fleet had their pick on payday; many fights broke out at closing time over which sailor would get which girl. Any farm boy seeing it for the first time remembered how the stud dogs would fight over a bitch in heat. We learned to talk drunk and fight sober. The Recruit Training Center was turning out hundreds of new men who were not given liberty until they finished training. Most of them wound up in the whorehouses in downtown Norfolk when they finally were granted liberty. This was the picture: You were let in by someone and led to a room where scantily dressed girls sat and talked to you until you decided which one you wanted. Once in the room with a girl you were checked for disease, paid your $2.00, washed with warm soapy water (more to excite you than for cleanliness), had your pleasure, and were shown out. Total elapsed time was not more than 30 minutes.

Most of the older sailors had *shack jobs*. When the government finally approved the Navy-dependent allotment, many of the girls who had been living with the sailors married them so they could draw the extra pay. At the same time, those who had never thought of marriage now married one or more sailors just for the allotment. Five allotments was the most I ever heard of one girl drawing. I don't remember how much time she served in prison. A girl like that had no worries unless more than one husband came home at a time. The Navy did not want you to get married before you had a rating high enough to take care of a family. You had to get permission to get married if you were low on the pay list. I can still hear the words of warning to us: "If the Navy wanted you to have a wife, they would have issued you one!"

One thing that caused bad blood between the Navy and civilian homeowners was signs in the yards of the finer homes that read, "Sailors and dogs keep off the grass." Many signs were vandalized or urinated on. I was high on the list of sailors who committed this friendly little act.

⚓ 2 ⚓

A BOOT IN
USS WASHINGTON

MARCH 1941 – DECEMBER 1941

On March 21, 1941, I received my orders to report to Philadelphia. The trip up from Norfolk was exciting. We rode to Baltimore on a ferry that was part of the old Bay Line System. I don't remember the name of the ferry, but I dreamed all the way to Baltimore about what a great sailor I was going to be. Then we caught the train into Philadelphia. When we arrived in Philadelphia, we rode by row houses built close together and owned by the people who lived in them for the most part. I thought they were a pretty sight. We also went by the stadium where Jack Dempsey had his big fight with Gene Tunney. On the way into the base, we could see many Navy ships. Exciting things were going on. Everything was humming and all the people were as nice as they could be. On March 22, 1941, I reported to the receiving station in Philadelphia to Captain R. W. Matheson, USN Commanding, for assignment to USS *Washington* BB56. *Washington* was one of the great new North Carolina-class battleships being built in those days. The keel had been laid down on June 14, 1938.

Upon reporting to the *Washington*, I was placed in the forward engine room to strike for machinist's mate and assigned to propulsion forward. The reason I was striking for machinist's mate was the beautiful red stripe all the firemen wore on their left shoulder. Also, firemen first class drew the same money as third class petty officers in other rates. We had no third class petty officers in "the black gang" (a nickname for engineers). Machinist's mate second class was our first eagle rating in the black gang. This was changed during the war. Later, when Commander Cochran broke me a rate for fighting, I became machinist's mate third class. I never tried for another rate, even though I stood throttle watches in later battles. If you could work that hard for a rate and have someone take it from you, I thought: to hell with the rate.

Since the ship was in dry dock, we slept in barracks ashore and only went aboard to become familiar with the layout of the ship while the construction work was being done. While we were waiting, we were assigned various things to do. One of my jobs was to escort dump trucks hauling magnesium from the Navy shipyard to Hunters' Point, just down the river. It was good duty and I learned something new each day.

A battleship is one of the most wondrous things that man has ever built. The average battleship shot 14-inch or 16-inch shells that weighed 2500 or 2700 pounds each. *Washington* was driven by four propellers connected to big General Electric or Westinghouse turbines. Firerooms were in separate compartments next to the engine rooms. They had huge water tube boilers using fuel oil, which was sprayed under pressure and atomized for efficiency to produce steam to 600 pounds of pressure and up to 800F. This steam went directly to the next compartment's turbines, which operated efficiently in a vacuum. Still in a vacuum, the used steam then went to the main condenser, which had hundreds of cooling pipes in a horizontal position with cold seawater forced into them from a big scoop under the ship. When we were not underway, a pump was used to force the seawater into the tubes. The cooled water was then pumped to a condensate tank and held at 112°F for reuse by the fireroom crew. The fireroom could also produce smoke in a battle situation, making it difficult for the enemy to see the target. The fireroom crew also produced auxiliary steam for the whole ship. Fifteen hundred men were aboard, and the ship would have been untenable without heat in the cold North Atlantic where saltwater from the waves froze before the next wave hit. Many times when we were above or near the Arctic Circle, ice built up on the decks, in the scuppers, and on the superstructure. Yet, the men below were comfortable in shorts and skivvy shirts, reading or lounging around their sleeping compartments when off duty.

Each ship is like a city, large or small. Even a tugboat is a little town all of its own. Everything that was done in the home happened right onboard the ship. The bakers baked, the cooks cooked, and the engineers ran the ship's propulsion division; the gunners, even on small tugboats, had machine guns and they learned to use them. All of this training is done after leaving boot camp. In the Navy, you specialize in a particular job unless you want to be a seaman and clean decks for the rest of your life. They assign you to be a striker in the area for which you are qualified. In the pre-war Navy, you had to learn quickly and well. If you didn't, you could not advance because the rates were awful hard to come by, and the Navy didn't waste time trying to train a man who wasn't learning.

Thousands of people were working in shifts in the summer of 1941 to get us down to the sea. Rush hour in the mornings and afternoons in downtown Philly was like nothing I had ever seen in my life. It seemed like the subways would never stop disgorging people. At the same time, another group going down into the subway would overflow from the sidewalk onto the streets. Rush-hour crowds contained the most people I had ever seen at one time.

If you were a sailor, you used the subway in Philadelphia. My first ride on a subway was with Machinist's Mate Second Class L. L. Denton. We went down a dirty stairway covered with cigarette butts and trash. At the time, it was shift change for the Navy yard workers. Going down the steps wasn't too bad, but the platform soon became very crowded. It was push and shove to get through the sliding doors into the train. The lights were bright. None of the people crowding around would even look at you. Women pushed and shoved as much as men; some men would sit down and read the afternoon paper while pregnant women stood nearby hanging onto a strap to stay upright. On this trip, we were going to Jenkintown where Denton's girlfriend lived. I was going to meet one of her friends. The cars took off and the lights dimmed. It was wilder than riding a mule with a sore back. I wondered why Denton wanted me to meet this girl, and I was worried. She turned out to be one of the nicest people I ever met, and we dated on many occasions while I was in Philadelphia.

Friendly shipyard workers invited us into their homes during this time. Also, both New York City and Washington, D.C., were close by.

While waiting for the ship to be commissioned, Charlie Fry, a first class water tender, started to teach me about the firerooms. In turn, I would buy beer for us at the base recreation room at $0.25 a pitcher. Charlie was married and had a hard time supporting his wife and kids. With his help, I was soon fireman second class and studying for fireman first class. He was a fine teacher, leading me through the forward engine room and fireroom and showing me the machinery while it was being installed. I came in contact with the first asbestos I had ever seen. Installers were wrapping it around the steam lines, molding it into a plaster, covering it with canvas, and painting it white. At that time, no one ever dreamed it would cause lung cancer. The little devils in the asbestos floated around as pretty as could be and they often came back to hurt you years later.

The company with the contract for hauling the magnesium from the Navy yard finally finished its job. The magnesium looked like coal. The company made money on the job and gave a big party for all the sailors and truck drivers. They had plenty of food and bartenders serving beer, wine, and whiskey. We had a good time and felt welcome in the city. Philadelphia was a most generous host. Wearing your uniform in the city assured you of a good time. You were real special, and the girls were too.

Just outside of the Philadelphia Navy yard was a big park with beautiful shrubs, flowers, trees, walking paths, and park benches. I spent many afternoons and early evenings there and met many nice girls. We met our girl friends for picnics in the park located by the Municipal Stadium. They went together like peas in a pod.

Somewhere in the city's more run-down section was a big derelict building with a bar in the second story called the Mid-City Club. It was exclusively for sailors and was a tough place to go. The girls there were tough enough to eat nails, even making us feel subdued at times. When a fight started, that old building would rock and roll. If you ducked under a table, you might not get hit. After a few minutes, everyone would sit down and start drinking again until another fight started. I never saw a Shore Patrol or cop in the place.

One of the bar girls invited me to come home with her at closing time. We walked arm in arm about two blocks and up a set of rickety stairs with dim, burned-out lights to the third floor. The communal bath was in use, locked from the inside. She ran up to her door and couldn't get it open fast enough. Inside, she had a pull-down bed to the left and a cooking area to the right with a single washbasin on the wall. When she reached the basin, she cocked her right leg up on it and let the used beer fly with me in line behind her. I was drunk enough that she didn't look too bad. The room was only half dirty, and the bed looked inviting. Needless to say, I went to the nearest pro station and worried for the next 21 days. That was the only time I went home with a Mid-City Club girl.

Our engine room turbines were so big they would have sunk a small island. The boilers were beyond a country boy's imagination. You could play around on the shaft of the propeller like kids play on a tree limb. The propeller was several stories high. I'd go down under the ship and look at the double bottoms designed to save you in case a torpedo hit. Then I'd go

around the ship and look at the 16-inch armor on the side of
the ship above the waterline. The deck also had three inches
of steel on it for protection from bombs. The superstructure
was pretty well-armored where the ship needed protection. Our
armaments in those days ran the gamut from "pom-pom" guns
to 16-inch gun turrets. The "pom-pom" guns were for anti-
aircraft fire and proved to be very ineffective. They were later
replaced by 40-mm mounts, the best anti-aircraft guns in Naval
service. We also had 5-inch twin mounts, some manned by
Marines, others by sailors. The 16-inch gun turrets were big!
One man couldn't handle a charge of powder. We couldn't put
the shells in by hand like we did on destroyers. We had to use
mechanical means in handling the 16-inch shells. If one of them
had ever exploded in Chattahoochee, it would have scared
everyone to death. The gunpowder in silk bags and the storage
rooms were the only things on the ship that counted; the storage rooms held the shells and gunpowder for shooting at the
enemy, an enemy that we didn't have yet in 1941. We were just
getting ready to fight.

This monster ship, the *Washington*, weighed 35,000 tons.
I doubt if any one man ever went into all the compartments.
She used fuel oil at an alarming rate. When we took on fuel,
it was like trying to fill the Grand Canyon with a hand pump.
The fuel oil king was usually a chief water tender or, on smaller
ships, a leading water tender second or first class. At sea, the
fuel oil king had to keep pumping oil from one compartment
to another as we used it to keep the ship's trim right. His job
was very important since he had to keep the ship in good trim
as we used up fuel oil and maintain records of the amount of
oil we used. Empty tanks had to be filled with saltwater for
ballast. The fuel oil king was also in charge of refueling at sea.
On these occasions, he was as nervous as a little red hen
penned up with foxes. Everyone on board was watching him,
including the Engineering Officer and Captain, who usually
gave unneeded advice.

Our freshwater storage tanks could flood a small town. All
the ship's freshwater was made from seawater and was as good

as any water I ever tasted. The evaporators were in constant operation. Our refrigeration plant was larger than any I had ever seen. We carried enough frozen food to last for months. The supply officer and storekeepers had to plan months ahead and provision the ship accordingly. Failure meant facing mad shipmates and an avenging captain. Our supply officers and storekeepers were good at their job because such failures never happened.

I became friendly with one of the leaderman riggers who had rigged and put in place our 16-inch gun barrels, which came into the dock on flatcars. Each gun was 60 feet long and weighed 108 tons. The barrels were set three to each of the main battery turrets, which weighed 1500 tons each with 16 inches of armor plate. The barbettes that received the guns had been milled to perfection. The rigger said he prayed continuously while this job was in process. Everyone else was glad when the mounts were put together and the 7-inch-thick gun roofs were finally swung into place.

The Marine contingent aboard ship served as landing parties, boarding parties, guard duty, and anti-aircraft gunners. In addition, they guarded "Officers' Country" 24 hours a day. "Officers' Country" consisted of the wardroom and officer state-rooms. The officers' wardroom looked like it covered an acre. After the war, I went aboard *Massachusetts* and could just imagine all the things that went on, such as officers eating and exchanging pleasantries and the captain at his table. I never did know much about that. I steered clear of "Officers' Country." The only enlisted people allowed there were stewards and steward's mates who acted as servants to the officers. Most stewards were either black or Filipino; and they were restricted to that rating, although they were allowed to help man the guns at General Quarters.

Our Captain, H. H. J. Benson, was very old. He was the son of Admiral William S. Benson. He seemed to like holding Captain's Mast and favored solitary confinement in the brig on bread and water with full rations every third day. I never went before him, but I truly believe he wanted to put the whole ship on "piss and punk" every so often for the good of the Naval service.

The closest most of us ever came to Captain Benson was at dress inspection. I worked for hours shining my shoes, brushing my uniform, shaving just right, and brushing my hair; then, I started all over again. The captain was the same each time; that is, he didn't notice me as a human being. He was only looking for good posture and the correct dress code, haircut, and shave. I hated that part of the Navy with a passion. It should be the duty of each officer to feel that his crew is human.

The Chief Master-at-Arms on a battleship is the right hand of the captain and serves the captain well in his climb to power. Our Chief Master-at-Arms had his quarters on the port side, forward part of our mess hall. It was finer than that of many senior officers. He and his cronies were always present, looking down their noses at mere mortals like us. Most of them were afraid to go ashore or mix with the engineers. We wouldn't take as much crap as the seamen. I disliked our Chief Master-at-Arms intensely. Suddenly, one day we noticed he and his gold service stripes, jaunty cap, and kiss-ass crew were gone! His quarters were found to be a homosexual hotbed. He had lost his retirement and been discharged from the Navy!

During those days, we set chairs and benches on the fantail and had entertainment by members of the ship's crew, including singers, bands, actors, and boxing. It was great fun to watch your shipmates do their thing. Afterwards, we had movies at the same spot complete with iced tea and lemonade. The funniest entertainment of all was when a big Marine named Fox boxed the smallest sailor aboard who weighed maybe 130 pounds. I think his name was Dittimore. Fox would lean over and Dittimore had to leave the deck to hit his chin. Captain Benson always came to see Fox and Dittimore put on their act and laughed all the way through.

While we were in Philadelphia, I used to go aboard the old *Olympia*, which had been Admiral Dewey's flagship at the battle of Manila Bay. It was tied up near the entrance to the

Navy yard. I'd sit on the deck and daydream. One day while I was there looking at the old round cannonballs stacked up on the deck and reading for fireman first class, Secretary of the Navy Frank Knox came on board and took a turn around the deck. He talked with me for at least ten minutes. Knox was extremely proud of the new ships being built in those days. This chance meeting was the only time I ever talked to him. After Frank Knox left, I had a sense of power and the awesome responsibilities ahead that I had never felt before. For the first time, I realized that *Olympia* had been a great ship in its day and that the ships we were getting were the best in the world. At the time, I didn't realize that the role of the battleship in the Navy would decline in World War II because aircraft carriers would make them almost obsolete.

Our Executive Officer was Commander W. P. O. Clarke. Good as an organizer and well-liked by the men and other officers, he came from tin-can duty having served on destroyers as well as battleships. He was one of those rare men born to be a leader. Our Gunnery Officer was Lieutenant Commander Walsh and in short order we became known as one of the best gunships in the fleet. Every ship needed a Lieutenant Commander Walsh since shooting was what it's all about. Lieutenant J. G. Ross was Assistant Engineering Officer in propulsion forward division. I learned much from him, and I am proud to have served under him. I'm sure he went on to better things in his beloved Navy.

Washington was finally fitted out and ready for sea. She was commissioned on May 15, 1941. The mix of sailors included about 60 percent of seasoned men; the rest of us were new sailors. I was dressed better for the commissioning than I had ever been before. My mouth was dry, and I could hardly speak. The officers, every last one, looked like gods in white uniforms. I was standing at attention in the group of engineers. From where I stood, I couldn't see a thing except water shooting up from the fireboats and tugs as we slipped out into the river. All kinds of speeches were made and bands played. We threw our hats into the air as tugs blasted out with foghorns. Everyone went crazy as we were launched, but our work was just beginning.

After the commissioning, we went dockside and started the process of getting ready to go on a trial run down the river to the freedom of the bay. We took on fuel oil, food, and drinking water. Cleaning up construction grime from the decks, doors, bulkheads, and living spaces had changed *Washington* from a cold steel hulk into the leading lady of our lives. As long as any of us are alive, that love will remain. We were eased into the river by tugs. With many of the construction crew still aboard to help us, we went on our maiden run. Many things went wrong, which were promptly written up and fixed on the run. Bigger problems were solved on our return.

One of the main problems was finding the proper screws for our driveshafts. When we went to full or flank speed, the ship would shake all over and yard workers had to do welding and bracing all over the ship until we found screws that worked. We changed screws every time we went to sea, trying to get the correct pitch and size. We finally found a set that worked for us.

On the ship, the new men kept getting lost for at least the first month, while the old salts did a little better at finding their way around. Even if the older men were lost, only their blank looks betrayed them. Instead, they would ask what division lived here and know where to go, while we new men didn't even know what a division was.

Our mess hall was on the port side below the quarter deck. (I knew how to find it.) All the coffeepots, soup kettles, serving trays, and steam tables were cleaned and polished better than a new bride's ring. It was here that we met our new cooks, bakers, master-at-arms, and an ever-changing crew of mess cooks. We all had to take our turn on the serving line as mess cooks; we worked at preparing fruits, vegetables, Irish potatoes, and onions. We also had to clean up after each meal and shine all the equipment in sight. Cooks, bakers, and strikers watched our every move and raised hell about cleaning up. At

times, a mess cook worked from 4:00 AM until 9:00 PM or
10:00 PM. In fact, they were called "galley slaves." I never
once caught mess-cooking and consider myself lucky not to
have had this duty.

When a battleship like *Washington* was in port and got ready
to put to sea, every man on watch had a job to do. First of all,
the duty watch in the firerooms had to raise steam. At the same
time, the electricians manned the switchboards. The engine
room crew was busy checking for leaks of any kind and lighting
off. The Chief Engineer and his officers were on pins and
needles while the chiefs watched everything. The deck divisions had to secure all movable topside equipment, dog down
the hatches, and man all seagoing watches. The Captain was
on the bridge watching everything like a hawk. His Executive
Officer was like a mother hen. The Boatswain's Mate piped
every order on his pipe and then followed it with a verbal order
on the loudspeaker, so everyone aboard was well alerted to
what was going on. The Captain's gig would come along
starboard and be hoisted aboard, and then the longboat would
pull up to the port side and be hoisted up and made seaworthy.
The portside ladder to the boats was pulled up and secured.
The rigging looked like a rainbow with signal flags flying.
Charts were laid out for the navigator. The anchor watch was
set in motion and the anchor was raised. On the bridge, everyone heaved a sigh of relief when we started to move. It was
like watching a birth to see a battleship come to life and start
to move. Anyone seeing it realized that a miracle was
happening.

Our living compartments were large, clean, and comfortable. The covering over the steel deck was fireproof in a semi-
safe way and kind of comfortable to walk or lie on. Our bunks
were just large enough to lie on and were covered with a fitted
sheet, a regular sheet, and a wool blanket. The bunks were
held by chains and separated by two steel posts to which they
were fastened. When you were out of the bunk, it was folded
upward to the post and fastened to give you more room. When
they were unfastened, you were only inches away from another

sailor. The bunks were in three tiers, so many men slept in a very small place. Bunks near the bulkhead stood alone, and I always tried to get one. Needless to say, if your bunkmate loved Navy beans, you suffered from gas as much as he did; only you were on the receiving end.

Our sick bay was tip-top in every way and staffed with good doctors and a fine surgeon. Our pharmacist's mates were well trained and could even take a doctor's place in an emergency (many did). Because of this fine group of doctors and pharmicist's mates, who often worked while fighting was going on all around them, many men who are alive today would otherwise have died.

Working in the engine room with Machinist's Mates First Class L. L. Denton and H. A. Cade was an experience never to be forgotten. Denton was from Texas. He was a good sailor and knew the engine room well. He tried hard to teach me; we crawled all through the bilges from bulkhead to bulkhead, learning the locations of all the steam lines and hidden valves. While teaching, he also made me laugh. He would pretend to be Hitler, giving speeches and saluting. He could also act like a Japanese. If you were ashore with him, you couldn't buy drinks because people kept putting them in front of us. Cade was tall and well built, and later made chief. He was as quiet as Denton was funny. He taught me about the turbines and pumps by using textbooks and the civilian experts who had overseen the building of the ship. These civilians spent many hours of their off-duty time helping us learn our jobs. We started to shape up as a unit. Every other division was in the same process. We learned in a hurry and ranged up and down the coast: Casco Bay, Maine; Norfolk, Virginia; Guantanamo Bay, Cuba; Haiti; and all over the North Atlantic. Everywhere we went, it was drill, drill, drill; target practice; and launch our seaplanes.

One day we moved to a secluded spot in Gravesend Bay to take on 16-inch projectiles. Two ammunition lighters came and tied up to us, one port and one starboard. The 2700-pound shell was landed on the deck on oak dunnage sloped to the center. Chains were passed under it. A heavy four-wheel cast-iron cart was pulled over it. The chains were positioned at each end and wrapped once around the shell, which was then raised with a hydraulic jack and fastened to the frame of the iron cart. The hydraulic jack was the only modern piece of equipment. Everything else was done with block and tackle. Even the carts were pulled with block and tackle.

During this time, *Washington* flew a signal flag called Baker. It was bright red and always flown when we took on explosives. We took on 200 or 300 shells for each gun mount over a period of 24 hours. It was slow and dangerous work. On one particular occasion, a chain holding the shell up to the cart parted, and the shell fell making a hell of a thud when it hit the deck. Captain Benson could be heard all over the ship as he raised hell about the damage to his teakwood deck. He almost always watched from the wing of the bridge and abused the officer in charge.

Birds at sea are common along the coasts of all land masses. We had a little sparrow come aboard once when we were in port at Hampton Roads. He stayed with us until we were far out in the South Atlantic. We fed him bread crumbs and he seemed to be OK until we fired the guns and lost him to concussion. Sea gulls were also common, but the one bird that stands out in my memory was a great black and white albatross. These birds change color and size in different oceans; we ran into them everywhere except the North Atlantic. Perfect in looks and flight, the albatross would cross our path in the center of the Atlantic or Pacific Oceans. Skimming over the waves two or three feet above the water, never above mast high to a ship, the bird's wingspan was ten feet at the greatest and five or six feet at the least. They must feed on topwater fish. I don't know what they do for drinking water. I never saw one flap his wings. They always headed into the wind and seemed to let the direction of the wind decide where they went.

We had two Kingfisher seaplanes that were shot off the battleship deck with charges of powder. The seaplane consisted of a heavy, well-built body, a float, a single engine, two wings, and a rear-seat machine gun. The planes carried two people: the pilot and an enlisted man, who served as gunner and general flunky. The enlisted man also took care of the radio and a lot of the work that had to be done while the pilot was busy. The seaplanes were used as spotter planes above our practice targets, for towing targets behind them for us to shoot at, and later as observation planes and couriers. These planes were stored on heavy launchers, carried parallel to the ship until time to launch when they were turned a few degrees from parallel; a powder charge then pushed the plane to 60 miles per hour before it left the deck. When they reached the end of the catapult, they were flying. Since they were float planes, they could land in a calm sea, and we could take them back aboard with a crane.

Most of the senior people we worked with were enlisted men. Chief Mondeair was chief of the engine room. Cade and Denton worked for him. These three men were by far the root cause of our getting underway when we did. They knew the engine rooms thoroughly. The Navy had pulled enough of the old-timers in to teach us youngsters; they did a very good job. We got the ship to sea and back again on the very first try. (I don't believe any of them thought they could do it with a crew as dumb as we were.)

Chiefs are what keeps the Navy going. They are a buffer between the officers and the men. They keep Navy traditions alive, leading both the men and, in many ways, the officers. Neither good nor bad, they are the lifeblood of the Navy. Without them, we would have been nothing. That 35,000 tons of steel and those 1500 men became a unified, whole, living, and breathing organism. Ninety-five percent of the credit has to go to the experienced chiefs and petty officers, the backbone of the United States Navy.

Later, after the war began, I found that many sailors were killed on the way to their battle stations. Even though they were going right into the line of fire, they would head in the direction of their battle stations to be of some use in the survival of the ship. The training that we went through in boot camp was the deciding factor in how great our Navy would be. If a man was late to his battle station, somebody, either enlisted men or officers, would call his hand. Being late wasn't allowed. Once, a new recruit was sleeping under the after gun mount when we were at General Quarters and about to fire the 16-inch guns. He slept through the call to General Quarters plus the warning standby to fire the main batteries. The concussion nearly killed him. He was sent to a shore-based hospital. Everyone had new respect for the 16-inch guns after that.

There were four engine rooms and four firerooms. When the *Washington* got underway, she was a big, heavy monster steaming through the water. The distance from the main deck down to the engineer's living quarters seemed like a mile. When we went to General Quarters, we closed all the hatches and dogged them down. They weren't opened for any reason unless an officer gave permission. My first battle station was in the shaft alley where the shaft goes out to the propeller. We had to watch for leakage around the propeller shaft and make sure it was cool. The shaft had packing with bolts to tighten to keep the water from coming through. The shaft alley was isolated and near the bottom of the ship. If you were topside and hurried as fast as you could, it would take you one or two minutes with everyone in your way to get to the shaft alley.

Watertight doors were everywhere in the ship. They were rounded top and bottom, made of steel, and had lugs on them. You turned a wheel in the center of the door to tighten them. At the bottom, there was a raised piece where the door fit. This piece was at least 18 inches above the deck of the ship and was the greatest trap on earth for a man's shinbones. Any sailor who ever went to sea ruined his shinbones when General Quarters occurred and he rushed to get to his battle station. It was something you avoided automatically after you banged your shins often enough.

My second battle station in *Washington* was the forward engine room, lower level, watching the pumps and the different controls and machinery on the lower level of the engine room.

It was another isolated position near the bottom of the ship. There were steam lines and pumps all about. The main condenser, which operated under a vacuum, transferred used steam back into water, which could be pumped to the boiler and reused as steam again to drive the ship forward. We had to trace all the lines on the lower level and know the location of every valve and what to do in case the pump went out. The Navy always had a backup for everything. If we didn't do our job, the people on the throttleboards couldn't do theirs. It was that simple. If the vacuum fell on the main condenser, the ship would just stop. You had to have vacuum of at least 27 inches to have the condenser work efficiently.

If a pump went down in the engine or fireroom, we had the spare parts aboard the ship or stationed nearby on a repair ship. We would send somebody over to get the parts from the repair ship and fix it. If something broke and needed welding, we had welders on the ship. The gunner's mates were the same. They knew how to tear the guns apart and put them back together again. There were officers trained in every phase of seagoing duty with enlisted men under them who were well-trained and did all the work. We learned to do and say everything the Navy way.

The Captain was the brains of it all. He gave orders that came down from the officers to the chief petty officers and from them right on down to the petty officers and sailors who were specialists in what they did. Orders were carried out just like clockwork; everything happened the way it should. The whole thing was mystifying then, and it still is today. If they built a new battleship and tried to man it without trained battleship commanders and men, it would probably take at least two years for them to learn to handle the ship.

We had quite a battle going between the sailors and the Marines on the five-inch gun mounts as to which group was the best shot. We started real slow and built up to 22 rounds per minute. All of us were ready to do whatever came up. If we got into a battle, we thought we could win it. Every man aboard was positive.

The main deck was armor plate of varying thickness topped by a teakwood deck, which the seamen kept shining with a holystone. I've had a love for teakwood ever since that time. Engineers would lay around on the deck in the South Atlantic after their watch and observe other people keeping the deck clean.

Each division had its little kingpin who ran that division and the enlisted personnel. He was always a chief and always a hotshot, whether he knew it or not, because he controlled all the enlisted men in the division. When some of the older chiefs and senior petty officers would gather around and shoot the breeze, it was awesome to listen. You learned what to do in almost any port, where the girls were, which bars were the best, which side of the street to walk on, etc. This information helped you come back in one piece. When we arrived in Sydney after the war started, I already knew where to go. Scuttlebutt in the Navy is a better source of news and information than *The New York Times* is for the city.

The Damage Control Officer was one of the most important men on the ship. It was his duty to have people see that every door and hatch were battened down tight so that water could be prevented from going from one compartment to another. This battening-down determined how long the ship would stay afloat in battle. The Damage Control Officer controlled everything on the ship that would keep it afloat. He managed repairs, and he had repair parties responsible only for damage control stationed throughout the ship. I thought then, and I still do now, that we probably had damage control as good as any Navy in the world.

Suppose I was topside and my engine room station was down in the bottom of the ship. When the battle alarm sounded, I headed for the nearest hatch, ran to the next hatch, and so on till I got to my battle station and relieved the man on watch there as quickly as I could because, if I didn't, he might be late to his station. Once you got to your battle station, you closed the door behind you and helped the man on the outside in the next compartment dog it down.

You didn't open that door up again until General Quarters drill was over or the battle was done. If you took a hit in your compartment, you could bet they wouldn't open the door and let you out. You died right there unless it was safe to open it.

The whole ship existed for one purpose, that is, to empty the guns at the enemy. We had 20-mm, 40-mm, five-inch 38, and 16-inch guns. A broadside from the 16-inch guns would move a battleship to one side. If the guns were firing over to port, it would kick the ship to starboard. It dimmed the lights and shook everything when the guns fired, especially if you fired a salvo with all the guns at the same time or one right after the other. Having seen the shells being loaded, you knew that something big was going out every time the guns went off. The men below decks never got used to the fact that those guns exerted so much pressure on that 35,000-ton ship. When they all fired, it was like being taken apart in the boiler rooms of hell. You could see motor mounts jump and steam lines move. If they hadn't put expansion joints in them, it would have broken the steam lines.

When we encountered rough seas, it was worse in the bow. Motion bothered you least if you were near midship because you got the least up-and-down motion there. *Washington* would take a long, slow plunge, and the whole bow would get covered with water. If you were topside, you could see the waves break; below decks, you could feel them.

The rougher the weather, the less fresh air we had. Water would run down the vents topside, and we couldn't run the air blowers as we normally did. The air would get foul, the decks seemed slippery, and the bulkheads would sweat harder. Your stomach would get a bit queasy. I never did get seasick, even on destroyers in a storm; but everyone had a queasy stomach during rough weather. The old battleship's slow roll is just as apt to make you seasick as the destroyer's quick, pitched roll. Seasickness is probably one of the worst sicknesses that can happen to a man anywhere.

In many ports, we would anchor rather than tie up to the

pier because the size and depth of *Washington* would not let us dock. When this happened, we had to go ashore in a longboat. It carried about 150 men. The longboats would drop you dockside, and it was up to you to get into town and back to the dock before liberty was over. Drunks were common in the prewar Navy; the real blowouts came when we anchored at a shallow-water port with lots of bars and few women. The only thing left to do was hit the bars and spend the pay accumulated from our trip to sea. Men always arrived early for the last longboat to reach the dock. Some were drunk, some were passed out, and many of them would fall into the water. Sick sailors would upchuck on others, which always started a fight. The Shore Patrol and the sailors, both drunk and sober, pulled drunks from the water. The ones made mean by whiskey would walk through the crowd waiting for someone to lean toward them. Then they would come alive with curses and rock the unfortunate drunk to sleep with one hard right to the jaw, after which they continued on their way, looking for others to cross their paths. The longboat crew hated dockside liberty parties because the ones passed out were often brought aboard in cargo nets. The liberty party was good therapy for the pent-up feelings of lonesome men; it got rid of old problems and started new ones.

The best way to get to meet the captain person-to-person was to do something a little bit bad or very, very good. He'd see you in either case. The officers would put you on report, take you up to the captain, and he'd pat you on the back if you were good and give you hell if you had done something even a little bit bad. Examples of bad behavior included being ten minutes late returning from liberty; fighting; being picked up by the Shore Patrol; or talking back to a senior petty officer or, worst of all, to an officer. We were kept on our toes by the threat of a court martial.

Some of the sailors were not as eager to go ashore as others. I was always a regular "liberty hog." One of the towns I liked best was Philadelphia. The people there seemed to love a serviceman more than other cities. Philly had all the sights you'd want to see. The Liberty Bell was one thing I really liked, and I visited it several times.

New York City was great, but it didn't seem to have the same love for the serviceman. You could take liberty in any one of the five boroughs, and it was like going to a different town each night. The people were nice. I knew many boys who lived there and went ashore with them and met girls from the different boroughs. I liked Brooklyn best of all and had a girl-friend there I was deeply in love with at the time. We would go to Coney Island·and ride all the fun rides or go to a live show and see actors waiting for a break as they worked. The shows didn't cost much and you could see comedians, dancers, and singers. Coney Island hot dogs were served by greasy-looking characters and were as good as any in the world. My girlfriend was Italian. Her mother was a great cook and she always asked that funny-talking boy her girl went with to have dinner.

At times I would go to Central Park and meet girls. It was fun to spend a whole day meeting new people, watching families at play, and watching boys and girls rowing on the lake. I'd also go to Sand Street, just outside the Brooklyn Navy Yard, and drink with some of the seediest characters in the world—hard women who had long ago lost the mothering instinct, shipyard workers on a drunk, merchant seamen from all over the world, and gang members who ended up in prison or dead while they were still boys. You could get the hell beat out of you there if you were not careful.

Once we anchored off Port-au-Prince, Haiti. The tide was not excessive and, in no time, bum-boats with native divers came alongside with one old man and two or three kids in each boat. They ate anything we gave them and dove for pennies and small change. Some of our people wrapped silver paper around washers that sank very quickly, causing the natives to dive deeply for nothing. At the same time, barracudas swam in the clear water but attacked none of the divers. The more sadistic sailors kept moving along the rail carrying the divers in range of the sewage from the enlisted men's head.

Port-au-Prince appeared very pretty, all white in the sun, causing me to go ashore when liberty was called. It was a mistake. Port-au-Prince was one big sewer; everything was filthy. People were urinating in one small stream that dumped into the bay while others washed their clothes in the same water. Little boys ran up and said, "Hey blue boy, want a woman? My sister good. My mother good. Come with me." Or they said, "My sister virgin, 12 years old, come with me. You see." It was the poorest and most vulgar place I had ever visited, yet some sailors used these poor natives. Rum and coke was $0.15 a shot. I went back to the dock and caught the next liberty boat back to the ship. Needless to say, venereal disease sent many men to the sick bay at that time. I never wanted to see another place like Port-au-Prince.

Pre-World War II Navy life was geared to naval service. Twenty-four hours a day you worked at your assigned shipboard duties, such as housekeeping, and at your professional duties, such as machinist's mate or quartermaster, with the faint hope of qualifying for advancement in rating. Everything counted. If you were late returning from liberty or stepped out of line in any of your professional conduct, it counted against your qualifying for advancement. Inspections were often. You had to be perfect or you were called on the mat. I knew many shipmates with 12 to 15 years in service who were seamen or third class petty officers, not because they weren't good but because the Navy didn't advance you that fast. All examinations were highly competitive; any black marks hurt you more than they should have. It worked well for the Navy in World War II because of a backlog of good, qualified professional officers and men who could be advanced swiftly. We had hundreds of junior officers and enlisted men, who were ready to advance in rate and train our new men as fast as new ships could be launched.

The officers were pushing hard for excellence in both men

and ships in the early 1940s, and it was increasing our aggres-
siveness. The average sailor would fight like hell with his fists
any time he was provoked. I came out pretty well in most of
my fights because of a high school boxing coach named John
Thomas Meadows. I was also a good size and pretty strong. By
and large, the whole Navy was turning into a mean force. We
had visions of getting into World War II, which had already
started in Europe, and there was talk about Japan's "divine
leader." It seemed like the whole world was getting ready for a
big dogfight.

Over in China, against largely unarmed and untrained
Chinese, the Japanese army was showing themselves to be a
first-class fighting machine. Although the Japanese forces were
fighting for real, the only training we were getting was with
dummy shells and towed targets; but we were getting pretty
damn good with them. A mean fighting mentality was being
developed by the sailors and the fleet. Later on, when sailors
were called on to fight with rifles ashore, they fought well.
Marines fought from the ship with the 5-inch guns and also
did well. The Marines proved themselves to be without parallel
in amphibious landings. We had all been forged in the same
crucible, which was the training the officers crammed down
our throats. It paid off. The pharmacist's mates of that day
were not looked on as real fighting men. They took care of
most of our sicknesses. Since these were largely venereal, we
called these men "shanker mechanics." The "shanker mechanics" also went ashore with the Marines in combat. They were
some of the bravest people we had in the service; many of them
were killed going over the battlefield looking for or helping the
wounded.

We also had a name for the Navy reserves. They were
"feather merchants." When we expanded the fleet, "feather
merchants" turned out to be one of our most valuable assets.
Another group of men were known as "90-day wonders." They
were reserve officers. Some of them were the best military
officers I've seen in my life. Most of the doctors we had were
young men just out of medical school.

War fever was evident everywhere. Hitler was expanding the war in Europe as fast as he could. Most civilians wanted to talk to servicemen and get our thoughts on current events. U-boats were starving England by sinking merchant ships and causing critical shortages in Blighty. Our country provided them with 50 World War I destroyers for submarine work.

In the North Atlantic on October 17, 1941, we lost 11 dead and 24 wounded on the USS *Kearny*, our first destroyer to be torpedoed in World War II. She was damaged but not sunk, and rejoined the fleet later. Survivors from *Kearny* were picked up by *Greer*, an old four-piper that shortly before had been the first destroyer to be fired on by the Germans. These events came in quick succession. We lost *Reuben James* on October 31, 1941 to a German U-boat with only 45 survivors from a crew of 160 men.

⚓ 3 ⚓

SHOCK AT DAWN

DECEMBER 1941 – SEPTEMBER 1942

On December 7, 1941, we were in Norfolk anchored in Lynnhaven Roads listening to the radio. I was by my bunk when the bombing of Pearl Harbor was announced. Everyone had expected war to start with Japan, but not in this way. Diplomats were still talking in Washington, D.C., even as the attacks occurred. This surprise attack seemed like the enemy was hiding in the church and killing worshippers as they entered.

I was surprised at the effectiveness of the Japanese attacks. In less than two hours, our Pacific Fleet battleships were all rendered useless. Before this event, one of the thoughts that had been prevalent throughout the fleet was that we could beat the Japanese in just a few weeks.

One of the cooks had his family at Pearl Harbor. I talked with him several times; he was almost crazy with worry. His mother and father lived just outside the city and his brother was on the battleship *Pennsylvania*. He was happy when he received a letter later saying they were all safe. On the day of the attack, he came down to our compartment with hot, buttered bread and we sat and talked about his family for a long time. We also talked about all the men who died without knowing what was happening when the torpedoes hit.

After the Pearl Harbor news, we felt subdued and uneasy. All the scuttlebutt was low key and as sober as if your own mother or father had died. There was no bragging or brash declarations. It was earthshaking. We asked, "What happened? How had their torpedoes run so true in the shallow water of the harbor? Why didn't our radars warn us of the approaching planes? Why did they bomb and go away with no damage to their fleet except for the self-destructing midget subs?" We were all thankful they didn't find and hit our carriers at sea or the fuel tank farms so vital to the fleet. If they had been destroyed, we would have been fighting from the United States instead of Pearl Harbor.

Before the attack at Pearl Harbor, the Atlantic Fleet had been in a state of jitters after the Germans started to torpedo our merchant ships. In later action, one of our destroyers had been sunk and two others had been hit by torpedoes. Our civilian population had responded well with a backup of volunteers for the armed services from every state in our great union. The shipyards and factories started to hire men and women who manned their stations in quiet determination and did fantastic jobs. I was surprised by the vigor with which 95 percent of the people responded after the attack. FDR was in the process of putting our house in order for great battles. A sleeping giant was moving toward action.

From their enlistment to December 7, 1941, the thoughts of all Navy men were on Japan and Germany. We worked day and night trying to be perfect in drills. Most of our work was daytime drills; we became very proficient in spotting, shooting, and sailing in formation. Our main batteries usually hit the towed targets by the third salvo during the daytime. The anti-aircraft guns shredded the target sleeves quickly, and we flew the Navy "E" for Excellence, proving we were good.

Our escorting destroyers were good on submarine drills. We were almost totally prepared for daylight action. However, the Japanese worked mostly at night using float planes and nighttime flares to put the enemy in perfect view. Their destroyers and light cruisers had the best torpedoes used in World War II, and their lookouts were trained in night vision. Our officers and senior enlisted men talked of "crossing the

T" on the enemy battleline. To understand this, imagine a capital "T." The long leg of this "T" is the enemy, steaming into the fight with only the forward guns bearing on the fleet, while the other ship at the top of the "T" is broadside with all guns bearing on the oncoming enemy ship. We were the best trained Navy in the world, capable of fighting a rerun of the World War I Battle of Jutland. The whole Navy had a "Can Do!" attitude that was as strong in defeat as in victory. We were invincible, unified, and ready to fight.

After Pearl Harbor, things happened in quick succession. The U.S. Congress declared war on the Japanese. The Germans and Japanese both declared war on us. Our training was over; it was time for the real fight. Since we were anchored in Norfolk, we had men on liberty and leave, scattered all over. Orders for all military men to return to their post were broadcast. Shore Patrols rounded up military men ashore and sent them to duty stations. "Officers' Country" looked like a disturbed swarm of bees. Lighters came with last-minute supplies. The sea detail had been set earlier and reported that we were ready to sail.

Before we sailed from Lynnhaven Roads, the battle alarm sounded. The voice of the coxswain came over the loudspeaker, "This is not a drill . . . This is not a drill." For the first time, the "flutter-willies" went to jumping around in my stomach at the sound of the General Quarters alarm. I grabbed my pants and headed for the engine room which was near our quarters. The doorhatch got my knee. That made the "flutter-willies" settle down a little. The first person I saw was Cade, who was checking to see that everyone was there. Denton was over on the throttleboard wiping the throttle. Mondeair was sitting in his usual spot looking calm. J.P. Little, a new boy on the block like myself, was running around checking bearing temperatures and taking readings on all the gauges in sight. It was the first time we had gone to the engine room looking for a real fight. Never again would I head to the engine room during a fight without those "flutter-willies" getting me.

On December 12 and 13, 1941, we were anchored at York

River. During this time a destroyer tied up to us. Rear Admiral J. W. Wilcox was piped aboard with sideboys and a 13-gun salute. His flag was broken out and run up as *Washington* became flagship of Battleships Atlantic. Our Assistant Engineering Officer, Mr. Ross, gave notice to his division to beware of the Admiral. Ross' face showed his opinion of the man who was feared by everyone. The Admiral was mean and nasty to all those he came in contact with.

Christmas Eve of 1941 at Hampton Roads saw us at anchor with battleships *New York*, *New Mexico*, *Idaho*, and *Mississippi* and carriers *Hornet*, *Wasp*, and *Long Island*. We were busy all the time. Cleaning rags and bright work polish was used by every division on the ship.

On December 27, we were lead ship as we sailed into the Atlantic followed by battleship *North Carolina* and carrier *Hornet* with three of the oldest four-piper destroyers in the Navy. It was a real "Mutt and Jeff" appearance if you ever saw one.

One of the strangest things at this time was that the ship couldn't have lights, not even a running light. That thought disturbed everyone. You couldn't go topside at night, and the people who smoked couldn't smoke topside. When you opened a hatch leading to the deck, you had to make sure that the lights were off. We had lights that were either red (port) or green (starboard) in all the passageways that gave off just enough light to let you get through.

I went topside and walked around on the deck a little before darkness on the day we sailed. The seas looked unfriendly. The destroyers were moving in and out and back and forth like kids playing a game. They gave you the feeling that nothing would get through that destroyer screen. The other ships didn't seem to count much. *Washington* was the queen bee of the group; everyone else was there to take care of us. We were there to deliver the enemy a striking blow with our big guns if the time came.

March 17, 1942, found us at Casco Bay, Maine. We had ships all around us. Carrier *Wasp* and cruiser *Wichita* were anchored nearby together with destroyers *Plunkett*, *Livermore*,

Madison, *Lang*, *Wilson*, and *Ellyson* of Desron 8. We had been formed into Task Force 39 and ordered to report to Commander-in-Chief, British Home Fleet. Heavy cruiser *Tuscaloosa* stood into port and anchored nearby. All our crew and officers had expected to go to the Pacific. We were not happy about this new duty, but we were ready to fight. I was pleased to get ashore in Portland and had a big lobster dinner, but I didn't get to meet any girls at all. The food was great and I walked several miles there. It was a most pleasant place.

On March 26, 1942, Task Force 39 stood out to sea; our destination was Scapa Flow, Scotland. Long, curling, white-capped waves hit us all day. Men on every deck were heaving. We had sandwiches for meals and made fun of the sick ones, laughing and talking about pork chops, eggs and bacon, chocolate cake, and "shit on a shingle." All this talk of greasy meals made them sicker. Some men had buckets, and others hung out close to the head, sat or lay on the deck, and grew much sicker.

On the North Atlantic, Condition Two (a state of battle readiness, Modified General Quarters) was set and all doors, hatches, and ventilators on the port side were dogged down and secured against seawater getting into our ventilation system. The air became putrid and the boots got sicker. Our long, heavy bow went deeper into the seas and came up slower. Our port side life buoys went swimming and never came back. Lifelines were strung on the main deck. Machine guns were secured. Even in *Washington*, we could get above main deck level, and then look down and up at the sea. It seemed to me that the gods of the north were all pissed off at us for invading their waters and teasing us before they destroyed us. During one 8:00 AM to 12:00 noon watch, the Boatswain's Mate of the Watch suddenly came on the loudspeaker causing all hell to break loose: "Man overboard . . . Man overboard." On the port side, all stations were manned; a head count showed all present and accounted for. Everyone went crazy until someone said Admiral Wilcox was missing. Several men swore he had been on the main deck. The Marine orderly on duty ran to the bridge to report Admiral Wilcox missing. A message from *Tus-*

USS Washington in long swells while transiting the mid-Atlantic, en route to join the British Home Fleet at Scapa Flow.

OFFICIAL U.S. NAVY PHOTO NATIONAL ARCHIVES

caloosa reported a man swimming strongly toward a life buoy. On the boat deck, the lifeboat was swung seaward on the davits when Captain Benson had them secure the launch. On *Wasp*, orders to launch four search planes were given. Three of the planes landed after a frantic search, but the fourth plane and two men were lost to the North Atlantic. By noon, we had a new admiral. Rear Admiral Giffen in *Wichita* had assumed command of Task Force 39 and we were back in formation sailing on our mission to Scapa Flow at a steady 18 knots. Our escorting destroyers were out of sight most of the time. We had a memorial service for Admiral Wilcox and all things returned to normal. The wind was at 40 knots for 10 days.

Our lookouts had to learn to identify German planes and warships. The 42,000-ton battleship *Tirpitz*, pocket battleships *Admiral Scheer* and *Lützow*, heavy cruiser *Hipper*, and a dozen destroyers waited for us. They were more than a match for the British, which was the reason for our attachment to the Home Fleet. On April 1, 1942, light cruiser *Edinburgh* met us and led us to Scapa Flow.

We stood in to Scapa Flow, guided by British pilots, and moored at a buoy. It was a vast harbor with continuous winds, flat countryside, and absolutely no trees. Heather grew everywhere, and coal was right on top of the ground in the form of peat bogs. Native homes were built from local stone into sloping hills. There were more ships at anchor than I had ever dreamed of seeing. Each one had a big barrage balloon with its umbilical cord attached to the ship below. Each balloon was trailing cables to catch enemy planes when they made runs on the ships. Admiral Giffen now had his flag in *Washington*. We wondered if the ghost of Admiral Wilcox would visit him.

As soon as we tied up, everyone aboard ship went topside. The water was full of surface ships while a vast, silent fleet lay at the bottom. The battleship, HMS *Royal Oak*, was one of the latest sunk. Almost every warship left in the German Fleet after World War I had been scuttled here by their German caretaker crews. We talked endlessly of the many ships rotting at Scapa Flow. What a historic place!

We stood out to sea for main battery practice. Our third

round made splinters of the towed surface target. We used 600 pounds of gunpowder and 2700-pound shells in this exercise. To my knowledge, we never had an air attack while we were at Scapa Flow. Shortly after we arrived, *Duke of York* led us out to sea for target practice. We outshot the British so badly it was embarrassing. We had visitors from every ship in the British fleet plus others who stayed aboard to study our new ship's boilers, engines, and power plants and the ways their design saved fuel. They were also interested in our expert gunnery. The British lived with our guncrews and were most devoted to their job. However, the English language as spoken by them almost kept us apart; we couldn't understand them. They were so different, yet devoted as shipmates and firm in their determination to win. His Majesty's Battleship *King George V* stood into port and moored with Sir John Tovey, Admiral of the Fleet, in all his glory. He was saluted with great military pomp. Tradition was half of the British fleet. Ashore, two British able seamen told me about the time when the battleship *King George V* had moved into a 10,000-yard range and gutted the *Bismark* with her 14-inch guns. They told me *Bismark* was red hot from fires in her compartments and went down with clouds of steam from the hot metal and massive explosions.

We all admired the British and they envied us for our modern ship and plentiful supplies. It was amazing to me how they stood in line at our ship's store for shorts, skivvy shirts, shoes, socks, and cigarette lighters. They also loved our food. Once, we received some sausage with cereal in it supplied by the English. There was no comparison between their food and ours. The British civilian population must have gone hungry at times. Our carrier *Wasp*, destroyers *Madison*, *Lang*, and British destroyer *Echo* stood out for Greenock on the Clyde where 60 Spitfires were loaded and delivered to the battle-scarred Island of Malta. Task Force 39 stood out to Pentland Firth for long- range anti-aircraft practice. After several hours, *Wilson* had a submarine contact. As the destroyers speeded in to attack, *Wainwright* had a torpedo pass her bow. The submarine left for calmer waters and we returned to Scapa Flow.

Anyone who ever went to sea admired the destroyers.

They were small and pretty as a greyhound running after a rabbit. They rode the rough seas like a rodeo cowboy rides his horse in a championship. When a destroyer passed near us, we waved to the crew as if to thank them for protecting us.

Most of our off-duty time on routine sailing days was spent below deck. We had duty stations that were ours to keep clean, and we enjoyed this task. It helped break the monotony of being at sea. My station was the coffeepot area. I would work on it and get to talk to anyone who wanted coffee. Chief Mondeair would come down and sit for most of a watch and leave right in the middle of a tall sea tale as if he had to go somewhere in a hurry. Maybe he had a call to the head. However, listening to him was very interesting.

When we were the long-distance covering force for the PQ convoys, we went to Iceland. Some of us got to go ashore at Reykjavik. We were amazed at the purity of the air and the way they heated their buildings. They had pipes going down into the volcanic heat generated underground. Iceland began as volcanic eruptions and had plenty of geothermal energy to heat everything. The people were pretty nice-looking; most of them were blonde. However, they were the most unfriendly people I ever ran across anywhere in the world. As a general rule, they had bad teeth and very rude manners. You could go to a store and they didn't seem to care if you were there or not. The one thing they had that I liked was good pastries, which were a bit sweet but better than the pastries available in the average store. I can also remember one tugboat in the harbor at Reykjavik tied up to a stone quay. It blew smoke rings just like smokers do.

I went through a lot of storms in both the Pacific and the Atlantic Oceans. If I had to pick which one was worse, I'd choose the North Atlantic because of the cold and prevailing icebergs. I worried about getting torpedoed or sunk and ending up in the cold water. The roughest seas I've ever encountered were along the coast of Norway and into Murmansk and Archangel. When I was topside in the superstructure looking down, I had to dodge back when a wave of 40 feet or more washed over

USS Washington *and British aircraft carrier in Scapa Flow, April 1942.*

OFFICIAL U.S. NAVY PHOTO   NATIONAL ARCHIVES

the anti-aircraft gun tubs on the fantail and ripped them away. Anything on the bow was beat up worse than that. A man's life expectancy was nine minutes or less in that raging hell of high waves, icebergs, and freezing water.

One machinist's mate second class slept near me. He wore two enlistment stripes and had been in the Navy about ten years in battleships. *Washington* was his home, and he was content to stay in his steel eggshell unless he had business ashore. All of his activities were aboard ship. He read, wrote letters, studied lessons from correspondence school, and enjoyed being in the Navy. People in other divisions were the same. Many of them went ashore only to get drunk, come back, sleep off the headache, and get back into their love affair with *Washington*.

I always loved to leave that world of steel doors, electric lights, and stale odors. I'd walk the deck stern to quarterdeck, clockwise and counterclockwise, up and down ladders to topside stations, always looking at the seabirds, flying fish, sounding whales, and playful dolphins. This ritual was as restful as a walk in the woods to me. One could make love to Mother Nature both at sea and on land, and it was great. I hated a battleship below decks and longed to go to destroyer duty where there was daylight in the engine rooms and every man was a shipmate, free to work and enjoy life.

While at anchor in Scapa Flow, we were able to go ashore and meet our English cousins, that is, those in the military. There were no civilians around. I kept looking for some Jernigans but I never found any. I found one McAlpin in the Scots Guards. (My grandmother had been a McAlpin.) I looked around for other family names, such as Colsens and Dolans, but McAlpin was the only one I found.

Many Scots Guards marched in the cold weather with their knees showing red and chapped. Everyone always wanted to know if they wore panties underneath the skirts—a sure way to start a fight. At Scapa Flow, there was a big theater for movies and beer halls where we would drink lots of warm British beer and gather around the piano to sing songs like "I've Got Six Pence," "Bless Them All," or "Bell Bottom Trousers," both

English and American versions. Some of the Irish tenors
brought tears to everyone's eyes. The memory of a Scotsman
with bagpipes playing "Danny Boy" still haunts my mind 50
years later.

We could go aboard any of the English ships in the harbor
in Scapa Flow. Aboard *Rodney*, most of the ratings slept in
hammocks and were divided into mess groups. One or two
ratings would go to the galley for the entire group's chow. Each
man also received a daily ration of rum, which was a tradition
with the English Navy. English sailors drew less money then
our Navy men and worked with much less up-to-date equipment, yet they were some of the most motivated servicemen I
ever met. I was amazed how easy our life was compared to
theirs. It seemed that the English didn't care as much about
comfort as our Navy. I believe we did a better job of handling
damage control problems than they did. Our older battleships
were more in line with theirs, but the newer ones like *Washington* and *North Carolina* were much more superior, and probably
superior to anything the Germans had.

King George came and inspected us in *Washington*. Everyone was excited about having the King look them over. We
were privileged to see him up close. He wore a Naval uniform
with the same insignia on his cap that all the world has known
since England became a household word. He was inspecting
us as if our forefathers had not taken the measure of his forces
at Yorktown. When he left, he signaled back to have a round
of grog for all hands. Of course, we couldn't do it since the
U.S. Navy is dry; it was kind of disappointing. I would have
liked to have found out what grog was. The Englishmen called
it Nelson's Blood, which goes back to their history when their
Admiral Nelson was killed and pickled in rum. King George
was a leader whom we respected. When he died after World
War II, I could say I saw him at Scapa Flow.

At Scapa Flow, I met an old fisherman when I was on shore
leave. I had seen a little fishing skiff going out to those rough
seas and wondered how the fishermen did it. He was the rug-
gedest looking guy I've ever seen. He looked like he might be

prematurely old; his skin was all wrinkled and his hair was grey. He would row right out in the big waves and go his way fishing, returning with fish to sell and eat. He lived in a house of native stone built into a hillside. He invited me home to dinner one day to meet his wife. They had lost one of their sons in a sea battle between the Germans and English and were heartbroken about it. Practically all their food came from the sea, except for what they absolutely had to buy from the store. Their fuel was peat dug right off the top of the ground. For dinner we had some very good fish. I became very friendly with them and went to see them several times. They were the only civilians I met while I was there. The last day before we stood out of Scapa Flow, we had a good fish dinner, but it made me sick. On the way back to *Washington*, I kept throwing up and may have had ptomaine poisoning. I was lying at the fork of the trail when some English soldiers went marching by. I heard one of them say, "Look at that bloody drunk Yank." I was so sick, I couldn't even wiggle my middle finger.

We never stopped at any port for long and were at sea most of the time after Scapa Flow. During these trips to sea when we were not on duty or at battle station, the men had to have something to do to relax. You became wiser standing around the coffeepot than a lot of people did going to school. You could learn every subject imaginable around the Navy coffeepots of that time. One of the best things to do was listening to scuttlebutt, which I have mentioned before. The radiomen put out the best information because they received all our messages. We knew about the sinking of *Prince of Wales* and *Repulse*; about Bataan and Corregidor; about the way the Japanese had run through the Dutch East Indies; and about the way the Asiatic Fleet had been whipped so quickly. We knew that the Asiatic Fleet had nothing to fight with. That was the same story for the first year and a half of the war.

Life aboard *Washington* was easy. We had good food prepared by fine cooks. However, after about six weeks at sea, we ran out of some foods and had to use supplies from the English. (Yuk!) We had entertainment supplied by our band. We could

King George VI inspects the crew of the USS Washington while at Scapa Flow. Note Kingfisher seaplane in background.

OFFICIAL U.S. NAVY PHOTO   NATIONAL ARCHIVES

run on the decks in fair weather, work out in the chow halls between meals, and participate in boxing. We had a good supply of books by Ernest Hemingway, Robert Service, Rudyard Kipling, Ralph Waldo Emerson, and Jack London. There were worship services and a chaplain to talk to at any time. Movies were shown below decks, but I didn't care much for them. Hollywood never understood a war and gave the people at home a false sense of security. Even with all the diversions, loneliness rode our shoulders like a lead weight. I especially missed seeing trees and flowers, taking a walk in the woods, or just lying in fresh-mown grass and looking at the sky as cloud formations floated by.

The sailors would huddle around in the compartments during bad weather and talk about the girls they had known and the bars they frequented. The group that congregated to hear the girl tales was probably a little larger than those who congregated to hear about a farm in Tennessee. Many men would just go into a passageway alone or lay in their bunks and daydream about home.

We had men called "sea lawyers" on the ship. They had been in all kinds of trouble and tried to beat the system. We also had people who were real smart about girls; we called them "cocksmen." Old-time sailors told us about liberty ports. Many times we would get together to talk about the ship and the places where we worked.

Another form of recreation was poker. We had poker games where the players would hide in a compartment to play. As the winnings grew, some of the games would have thousands of dollars in them. There were also crap games where the crap table was painted right on canvas just like a professional table. I've seen as much as $20,000 at one table. It was full of crapshooters and cardsharps. The two-dollar bill was the usual unit of pay. With everybody at sea now for five, six or seven months, we had all drawn a little money. That little bit of money crept into the hands of maybe 20 percent of the ship's gamblers. Some of the games staggered your imagination.

One thing everyone seemed to talk about in almost any

conversation was the German battleship *Tirpitz*, which was at Alten Fjord. If it was there as a psychological weapon, it was a good one, keeping the British Home Fleet plus the American warships standing by in case the German ships came out to fight. I didn't know what the British were doing to the German submarine forces, but between January 1, 1942, and July 14, 1942, the United States had only sunk eight German submarines. It didn't seem that we would improve much any time soon. In that same period, we had lost 350 merchant ships to the Nazi submarines for a total loss of 2.25-million tons. The Germans had sunk ships from Maine to Texas in sight of the people ashore. It's staggering even now to think about it. Riding over the water then, one couldn't even begin to imagine how many million tons of ships and equipment had gone down. The losses were beyond my imagination and soon changed for the U-boat sailors. Of 40,000 German submarine sailors, 30,000 would lose their lives in the battle of the Atlantic.

On April 28, 1942, we were changed from Task Force 39 to Task Force 99. The Pacific fighting was much on our minds. On April 29, we stood out to sea. The seas picked up as we passed the Faro Islands with mines floating loose all around us. We could hear depth charges in the distance. We received additional ships as British destroyers *Punjabi*, *Uribi*, *Martin*, and *Marne* joined us. Dense fog rolled in and the heavy ships all used fog buoys towed on 600-foot lines to maintain station. The buoys caused rooster tails of water as we steamed in line formation 200 yards behind the rooster tail put up by the buoy of the ship ahead.

On May 1, 1942, we were steaming in line behind *King George V* at 17 knots when *Punjabi* tried to cross in front of *King George V*. The huge battleship cut her completely in two. Half of *Punjabi* came down each side of *Washington*. Destroyer *Martin* shot through between *King George V* and *Washington* and carried away the buoy cable. Depth charges from *Punjabi* went off under *Washington*, knocking out circuits all over the ship. All motors shut down and the emergency motors came on line. All 1900 tons of the number 2 turret jumped the track. The range

finder went out and two-thirds of all the light bulbs were broken. The after-steering engine room crew was so badly shaken
by banging steel doors and radical steering that they got out in
a hurry thinking we had been torpedoed.

J. P. Little and I were in the shaft alley with the hatch
dogged down tightly. Little had the headset and didn't say
anything. As the bow went deeper, the screws came out of the
water while exploding depth charges drove us high in the air.
We finally began to settle by the stern and felt like we were
falling. The screws ran away until they bit into the water again.
The drive shaft started to leak, and I tightened the shaft packing with a special wrench. The leak stopped. Our reactions
were calm, but I think we both had to pee real bad. That
explosion was larger than any I heard during the remainder of
World War II. Meanwhile, four officers were dead on *Punjabi*,
but everyone else survived. It was the quick reaction from the
destroyers that saved many lives that day. *King George V* had 40
feet of damaged bow to be repaired. We departed Scapa Flow
for Hafnarfjordur, Iceland, for fuel, supplies, and repairs. Our
diver's examination found no damage to the ship's bottom. We
had liberty at Reykjavik.

When we crossed the Arctic Circle, they gave us a polar
bear certificate. I've lost mine over the years and wish I had it
today. It was about the size of a sheet of paper and told where
we had been.

Something that was quite noticeable in those cold North
Atlantic waters where anything could freeze was the Gulf
Stream. Every once in a while we would hit it, and the vacuum
in the main engines would go down to maybe 27 inches. When
we were in real cold water, it would get up near to 30 inches.
You could always tell by the way the vacuum dropped.

Pink-looking jellyfish were also prevalent in these waters.
The scoop for the main condenser picked these up by the
millions together with anything else in its way. Every time we
anchored, we had to drain it, get the jellyfish out, repair any
tubes that were stopped up, and plug the ones we couldn't
repair. These jellyfish were full of stingers. You had to wear

rubber boots and gloves or get stung. I've never seen anything as pink as they were. Once when I was on cleanup duty, we took the inspection plate off and I went in to clean the tubes. The outside man plugged the drill I was holding into the socket and the doggone thing had a short in it. I was standing in water about knee-deep when it hit me. I received quite a shock and began shaking all over. My helper started yelling; he didn't know what to do. One of the chiefs, I believe it was Chief Cade, came dropping down the ladder real fast and unplugged the drill. I came out so fast that I cut my back on the bolts that held the inspection plate on as I straightened up too quickly. It was an eerie feeling: an enclosed place in the bottom of the ship with those pink jellyfish all over everything, a drill in my hand that wouldn't quit turning, and a shock that wouldn't stop. It was about as scared as I have ever been in my seagoing life.

Our Senior Chief Machinist's Mate Mondeair was king of the hill in propulsion forward. He was a great big guy with a round belly. He never did seem to bother anyone, but I crossed him up around the coffeepot one day. He thought I was drinking out of his coffee mug and got all over me. Being young and of unsound mind, I yelled back at him. I was then told I would dive bilges. (To dive bilges, you had to go down under the floor plates and clean up.) I said, "I won't dive bilges." But he exerted his authority and put me in the bilges, and I worked until he said stop.

In calmer weather in the North Atlantic, the fog would roll in, and you couldn't see a friend, a bulkhead, or a stanchion an arm's length away. Then suddenly you would get an open space and be able to see everything for a distance of a quarter of a mile. The most awesome feeling was to be at one of the forward 16-inch guns sailing along through fog hearing the bow wave. You felt totally alone as you looked up to where the bridge should be. When the fog cleared away for a second, you could see the 5-inch gun mounts whirling; and you might see the captain's face peering out through the portholes on the bridge. It made you feel insignificant. You could go to the railing, put your hands near a stanchion to keep from washing overboard, look out, and see nothing but fog. You didn't trust anything when you were sailing with convoys because you knew there were at least 20 to 30 ships in the merchant convoy, plus the British and American warships.

Some of the least acknowledged people who served during World War II were the merchant seamen who went on those runs through the North Atlantic to Russia. They had one chance in three of coming back at all. There was no chance of living if they were sunk and weren't picked up immediately, which was unlikely. Anyone who went to Murmansk or Archangel was very, very lucky to come back alive. We saw the ships loaded to the waterline with goods in the hold and on the deck. We saw train engines, guns, tanks, and planes. You name it, and we saw it lashed to the decks of these merchantmen.

On June 27, 1942, PQ17 stood out of Iceland for the Russian ports of Murmansk and Archangel. It was the most ill-fated of the North Atlantic convoys. Assembled at Hafnarfjordur, Iceland, the 37 merchant ships were loaded with enough tanks, guns, jeeps, trucks, planes, and mixed cargo to equip 50,000 troops. The value of these goods was more than $100 million. PQ17 was closely supported by six destroyers, four corvettes, two anti-aircraft ships, three minesweepers, four rescue trawlers, and two submarines with a Royal Navy Commander riding in destroyer HMS *Keppel*. There was also a close covering force under Rear Admiral L. H. K. Hamilton of the Royal Navy consisting of cruisers HMS *London*, HMS *Norfolk*, USS *Wichita*, and USS *Tuscaloosa* with escort destroyers *Wainwright*, *Rowan*, and *Somali*. The long-distance covering force for PQ17 consisted of battleships HMS *Duke of York*, USS *Washington*, and HMS *Victorious*. This force also included heavy cruiser *Cumberland*, light cruiser *Nigeria*, and eight escorting destroyers.

When the British Admiralty thought the German Fleet was at sea, all the escorting ships were called back to intercept the German ships that were safe in Norway. Only 11 of the 37 merchant ships ever reached Russia. Pulling us back was an incredibly stupid thing to do and someone should have been relieved from duty and court-martialed.

We received orders to leave the North Atlantic area in August 1942. While at sea we got bits and snatches of the war news. Navy-wide scuttlebutt told us the disastrous things that had happened to us in the Pacific and to our Fleet. Although we all realized that getting the material to Russia would help win the war, I think every man aboard wanted to go to the Pacific and fight. It was a happy day when we left the Home Fleet and headed to New York City.

After arriving in New York and tying up to a pier, we all enjoyed liberty and a lot of fun. Sometimes I think it was probably the best liberty I ever had because I knew New York and liked to be there. I had claimed a lost liberty card earlier and kept it while a new one was made, so I had a liberty card in my wallet at all times. Another way of getting more liberty was through what I soon dubbed the "shit-can liberty." Most Navy piers had a head right on the dock that everyone used and trash containers for dumping trash from the ship. I already had a liberty card, so I'd fill a trashcan, wrap up my uniform, and put it in with the trash. After dumping the trash, I'd step into the head, slip into my dress uniform, and go just outside the gate where I'd have a few suds or see my gal. Then, I'd return to the ship in a few hours back in my dungarees with my dress uniform in the can. It was hard to keep a good man down!

After taking on stores, ammunition, and fuel, we anchored in Graves End Bay in September 1942. Many men had been transferred to new ships and new recruits had come aboard; many of them were married with wives in California, Texas, and elsewhere. I was not married but loved girls, whiskey, and liberty as much as any man. So when word was passed that only married men had liberty, it made me mad. Everyone who was single and had been to sea was mad as hell with the Navy and that stupid order because all of us wanted to go back ashore. These married boots were going ashore even though most of their wives were elsewhere while we, who had been fighting, had to stay on board.

Understanding how a person felt when he received this inhuman treatment, you would have to have been at sea for many months and have someone else be given an advantage over you like that. I went to rolling my dress blues, getting madder and madder, and before I finished rolling them for storage, I decided I would go ashore anyway! I got some cellophane and wrapped my blues, shoes, and wallet in it and put on my bathing suit. When I was doing this, another boy named R. I. Miller came up and asked what I was going to do. I told him, "Swim over to the beach and get liberty and come back." He said, "I'm going with you." So he ran and got ready. We went up just about dusk, popped off the fantail of the battleship into Graves End Bay, and started swimming toward the beach. There was the strongest tide I have ever encountered in inland water. We were swimming as hard as we could swim and weren't making any headway against the tide.

Fighting to get ashore, we almost gave up several times. We stayed together and got to the channel markers where we could hold on and rest for a minute or two, but the tide was pulling at us and the barnacles on the markers cut our feet and hands. Most of the time, we just kept swimming. We finally came ashore at Coney Island after dark. We never encountered any of the shoreline guards. We put on our dress blues, went ahead, and did our thing. He went one way and I went another. On the next morning when I got ready to go back to the ship, I went to the dock to catch a launch out to the ship, but the ship was gone. I didn't know what to do so I asked the Shore Patrol where I could go to turn myself in. He said the best thing to do was go to Pier 92 and, if I went by myself, it would be better for me. He was one of the very few decent Shore Patrol members I ever met. These people always fought to stay ashore, and if they were good to anybody, the Navy would ship them out to sea. I went to Pier 92 and turned myself in. The lieutenant who was Officer of the Day at Pier 92 asked me why

USS Washington *at anchor off New York City prior to the author's unauthorized swim ashore.*   OFFICIAL U.S. NAVY PHOTO NATIONAL ARCHIVES

I had left the ship like I did. I told him and he couldn't believe it. He checked a map and said, "My God, it's 11 miles from where you were anchored to Coney Island's closest beach." I don't know if that was right or wrong, but if it was, we had swum a long way. I decided I didn't want to be where I was, and I was very angry at the asinine order stopping us veterans from going ashore for some recreation while boots who had been in the Navy eight or ten weeks could go where they wanted. I didn't think it was fair then, and I still don't.

Pier 92 was one of the worst experiences in my Naval career. There were people from all walks of life who had been drafted and then went over the hill. There were murderers, homosexuals, transvestites, any kind of person you can think of in that brig. They just threw everyone in the same cell block. Anything could happen to you there. Those people were bad enough in the daytime, but at night they were something else. I could stand my own with most of them; the others didn't want to try me out. I knew I couldn't catch *Washington* and found out later she was bound for the Pacific. I wanted to get out of there so badly that I volunteered for any sea duty I could get. I was lucky. In a few days, I was interviewed and asked if I wanted to go to a destroyer. I said, "Yes Sir, I'd like to go to anything to get out of here." Pier 92 was my one and only look at a Navy brig. On the next day, eleven of us from the Pier 92 brig reported to the Brooklyn Navy Yard where we had been assigned to a newly commissioned destroyer, the DD465, USS *Saufley*.

⚓ **4** ⚓

DESTROYER DUTY

SEPTEMBER 1942 – DECEMBER 1942

Saufley (DD 465) was laid down on 27 January 1942 by the Federal Shipbuilding and Dry Dock Co., Kearney, N.J.; launched on 19 July 1942; sponsored by Mrs. Helen O'R. Scruggs; and commissioned on 29 August 1942, Lt. Comdr. Bert F. Brown in command.

Following shakedown off northern New England, Saufley *made several coastal escort runs and then prepared for duty in the South Pacific. She departed Norfolk on 9 September. Arriving at Noumea, New Caledonia, on 2 December,* Saufley *commenced participation in the Guadalcanal campaign three days later.*
—*from* The Dictionary of American Naval Fighting Ships

T he first time I saw *Saufley* she was tied up to a pier in Brooklyn Navy Yard. It was early September 1942. Shipyard workers were rushing to finish last-minute jobs. I thought, "This ship is going to be something special in my life." Although I had been in the Murmansk-Archangel convoy runs for many months, I was still just a prisoner coming from the brig to a new ship. I was fireman first class when I came onboard *Saufley* and wanted a break from the Navy for at least part of the night. I was broke. I tried to find Mr. Cochran, the Engineering Officer. He wasn't around. So I went to the Executive Officer's cabin. He wasn't aboard. I took a deep breath and went straight to the Commanding Officer's cabin and knocked. When Commander Bert Brown opened the door, I asked for liberty and a $5.00 loan. I got the liberty, but I didn't get the loan; he seemed upset that I would ask him. Back by my sack, I was getting ready to go ashore and Chief Water Tender Jim Knight strolled up, handed me $5.00, grinned and walked away. At that very moment, Commander Brown had my loyalty forever and, by sundown, Sand Street had his $5.00.

Saufley would be my home for over three years until the Japanese surrendered. It was a stroke of luck. I felt very lucky to have jumped overboard from *Washington* and then be able to get in *Saufley*. I loved her with all my heart every day I was ever in her.

The greatest thing about serving in a destroyer was that we lived so close to nature. Schools of porpoise would come alongside, adjust their speed to ours, and seem to play beside us like kids. They were unsurpassed as swimmers. Flying fish would land on the deck during the day and we would throw them back. Many of them died on the deck at night, and the seamen had to return them to the sea the next morning. Every time we passed a school of flying fish, we could see the larger fish trying to catch them. They swam so fast that, all of a sudden, they would break the surface with their fins extended and go from 25 feet to 50 feet or more. If these fish were facing a light breeze when they cleared the surface, they seemed to go much farther. It was a great case of survival of the fittest, the law we lived by.

From the ship's bow, which was maybe 18 feet or 20 feet above water, you could watch the destroyer cut through the water like a hot knife through butter. The salt spray would hit you in the face together with the fresh sea breeze; you would get a feeling of freedom that few people ever knew.

The destroyer sloughed off in height from 18 feet to 20 feet at the bow to maybe 6 feet at the stern where most of the off-duty crewmen spent much time shooting the breeze, reading, or just staring out to sea. When we were steaming at slow speed and speeded up, we could feel a surge of power as the screws bit into the sea and the ship's wake churned into a wide

USS Saufley pier side at the Brooklyn Navy Yard, September 1942, fitting out for the Solomons.

OFFICIAL U.S. NAVY PHOTO

froth. The bow would move like a fine horse about to run a race. The smoke from the stacks would change color where the added fuel oil met the forced draft air at the top of the burner as the duty fireman adjusted to the new call for power. We all rode in a great lady that answered any call to duty. She'll never die in our memories as long as one of us lives.

Saufley's hull number was DD465. She was named for Lieutenant (jg) Richard Coswell Saufley who was killed in an attempt to break his own altitude and endurance record in a Navy plane on June 9, 1916. He was the fourteenth naval aviator to receive his wings at the Naval Academy in June 1913. The ship was christened by his wife, Helen, on June 19, 1942, at the Federal Shipbuilding Yard, Kearney, New Jersey, and placed in full commission at the Brooklyn Navy Yard on August 29, 1942. Saufley Field at Pensacola, Florida, is also named for this aviator. Still in commission today, Saufley Field is dedicated to training Navy flyers.

Comparing the confined feeling of a battleship with its huge size and the freedom found in a destroyer within its smaller structure is impossible. I was born to be a destroyer man. I liked battleship duty, but I wanted to be in a destroyer. I have the greatest respect for the people who trained me in the battleship, including Chiefs Mondeair, Cade, and Denton; Lieutenant Ross; and all the others. I will forever thank them because I was able to go to *Saufley* and could have lit her off by myself. She was just like *Washington* except she was smaller.

We had a great mixture of men in *Saufley* that you would never find again on a new ship going to sea. Only 30 percent had ever been to sea before. The rest of the crew were civilians who had joined after Pearl Harbor. The crew consisted mostly of men between 17 years and 22 years of age. Probably no one was older than 42 years. Most of the crew were Italians from the New York City area. We also had people from Texas, part of the group of 1000 people who had enlisted and been sworn in on the same day and time in Houston, Texas, to make up for the lost crew of the cruiser *Houston*. Our regular Navy crew included good officers and chiefs. The enlisted men included

Asiatic Fleet survivors, men from the brigs, and hard-to-control men from almost any other area in the Navy. They all liked whiskey, girls, and liberty. The new volunteers were ours to mold, and we molded them in the same fashion we had been molded. They turned out to be some of the best sailors who have ever sailed the seas.

October 1942 was spent on shakedown training in the Casco Bay, Maine, operating area. We worked four hours on and four hours off in the engine rooms and firerooms trying to get our green crew ready. They were young, they wanted to learn, and they were eager to fight. Our Commanding Officer, Commander Brown, was a practicing Mormon who had worked at the Aberdeen Proving Grounds in Maryland with 5-inch 38 guns. Although he would never let us forget that it was our duty to destroy Japan and Germany, he'd pray for the souls of their dead at the same time. *Saufley* was a lucky ship. We were lucky in many ways, but most of all, we were lucky to have Commander Brown, a man born to lead other men, as our first Commanding Officer.

Our Executive Officer was Lieutenant Commander Tom C. Phifer, whom we immediately called "Scratchass." He would be talking to someone, and then he'd reach back and scratch his backside as hard as he could. He'd walk over to anything he could put a foot up on, get a happy look, and go on up to where the sun didn't shine looking happy as a new pup in the sunshine while he scratched away. He had that undefinable quality that made men want to do his bidding. We were lucky to have him to help us get ready for the hell to come. Soon after we reached the Pacific, he was transferred to a new destroyer escort as Commanding Officer. What a loss! "Scratchass" was a fighter and we all knew it.

Lieutenant Dale E. Cochran, our Engineering Officer, was a technician with no recognizable qualities of leadership; he just grew on you. His petty officers were all good men. They came from ships that had been sunk and from brigs Navy-wide. Some were survivors of the Asiatic Fleet's destroyers. All of them were cantankerous and prone to drink and fight. Cochran really did get the best out of us. Everyone cussed him, but no one wanted to transfer to other ships to get away from him. He was with us until 1945 serving as Engineering Officer, Exec, and Captain. A better officer never went to sea for the U.S. Navy.

Saufley was a 2050-ton ship, 376½-feet long, with a crew of 310 to 340 men. She was armed with five 5-inch 38 guns, five 40-mm twins, and 20-mm guns scattered all about the ship. Her ten 21-inch torpedo tubes also contributed to our fighting ability. We were a floating gun mount that could move fast, maneuver well, and fight like hell.

The ship carried a total of 100 tons of explosives. Our small arms started with the .50-caliber Browning automatic. Then we added the .30-caliber hand-held tommy gun, bolt-action rifles of World War I vintage, and .45-caliber pistols worn in holsters. These arms were for landing and boarding parties, and for use in any operation at close quarters, including shooting the enemy in the water and on the beaches when we were close enough. Monkey Point at Corregidor was a good example.

Our ship's guns began with the 20-mm Oerlikon, air-cooled automatic anti-aircraft gun whose explosive projectile boasted a range of up to 4,000 yards. This anti-aircraft gun had a peep or ring sight and shot 450 rounds per minute. It fired tracers to show the gunner his direction of fire and help him adjust to the roll-and-pitch of the ship. Many good gunners were prone to use the tracers more than the sights to get on target. The 20-mm gun crew consisted of the gunner, who aimed and fired the gun; the trunion operator, who raised and lowered the horizontal height of the gun so that the gunner, who was strapped in, could stay in an aiming and shooting position even to rotate 360 degrees as his target moved; the range setter, who fed the data into the gyroscopic sight; and two loaders.

Our 40-mm guns were Bofors, twin and quad-mount anti-aircraft guns with the strength of a cannon and the speed of a machine gun, firing 160 rounds per minute with a range of 2,800 yards. These guns had electric hydraulic systems and a remote control operation. With a fire control director, the crew had a trainer, pointer, mount captain, and four loaders. The shells came in clips of four. This gun could also be fired manually, but that made it less effective. The 40-mm gun is the Navy's largest machine gun.

Our main battery consisted of five 5-inch .38-caliber dual-purpose semi-automatic guns used for anti-aircraft fire, shore bombardments, and surface targets. These guns were the Navy's best. Our own captain had helped test-fire and write specifications for them at Aberdeen Proving Grounds in Maryland. When shooting at planes, we used proximity shells which were the best anti-aircraft shells in the world. Shipped to us after we arrived in the Solomons, they were set off by a magnetic field as they arrived in a predetermined area nearest the plane. Bang! No more plane! At first, the Navy wouldn't let us shoot them over an island fearing the enemy would find one intact and learn how they worked. Soon, however, we were shooting them anytime we had contact with a plane. We used anti-personnel shells for troops ashore and armor-piercing shells for ship-to-ship battle and bombardment before landings. Each mount had a pointer, a trainer, a fuse setter, a hot-shell man, a projector man, a powder man, and a gun captain. Right below in the handling room were four men to handle the shells and powder. Below that was the magazine with four or five men to pass up the powder and shells. A good crew could fire 22 rounds per minute.

For submarine work, we had "K" guns that shot depth charges to the port and starboard sides of the ship in patterns. Each charge weighed 300 pounds. At the stern of the ship was a raised rack of tracks made of angle iron and slanted to the stern. Six hundred pound charges were loaded in the rack at all times ready to go. The sonar man told the depth-charge crews at what depth to set the charges to explode. When the ship made a run over the submarine's location, the restraints holding the charges in place were removed and they rolled off the ship as we passed over the submarine.

Our torpedoes were 21 inches in diameter and were on a

raised deck fore and aft of the after smokestack. The torpedoes were stored in, and shot from, two banks of tubes, each holding five 21-inch torpedoes. This area was called the torpedo deck. Each bank of torpedo tubes had a mount captain, a gyro setter, and a mount trainer to aim and fire these weapons. We could fire to both port and starboard at the same time. The torpedoes operated and ran on a gas turbine system at a preset depth and a speed of 46 knots, firing to a distance of 4,500 yards. The explosive head contained 500 pounds of TNT. Toward the end of the war, later models with a much improved system had an explosive charge containing 1,100 pounds of torpex.

A typical day on the shakedown cruise consisted of all hands posted to General Quarters at dawn and dusk to guard against submarines, planes, and surface craft. We worked four hours on and four hours off. The ship had steam lines everywhere, many of which leaked and required immediate repair; and there were other minor problems. We also had calls to General Quarters several times each day and night to train the men on their General Quarters stations. With the shortage of experienced petty officers and with 70 percent of the men untrained, the burden fell like lead on our young but experienced shoulders. I really felt sorry for the new messenger boys who had to find us, wake us up, and sometimes take a cussing after finding their way along in the dark over the pitching, rolling deck from the engine room to our bunks. Most of them were a little seasick, but the only way to learn was to do. They did well and asked all kinds of questions. I worked mostly with Rudolph Einhorn and Ray Elliott, both of whom were older than I was. Elliott started to call me "Sea Pappy."

The forward engine room coffeepot was by the throttle board. It was handmade by George Abner Stoneham from Rose Bud, Texas. Instead of electricity, it used live steam and small coils for heat. We could put coffee grounds in the water and have it at a rolling boil in just a few seconds. The coffee made in this pot was the best I have ever tasted. Everyone drank lots of coffee. Each man had a cup as soon as he came on watch. It was always kept full by the messenger of the watch, and a

USS Saufley during shakedown cruise off the East Coast. Despite the camouflage paint, a green ship with a green crew.

OFFICIAL U.S. NAVY PHOTO   NATIONAL ARCHIVES

new pot was made for the men coming on watch. I am sure the outcome of the war was not affected by our pot, but it helped our morale a lot. Coffee was never in short supply.

Mr. Cochran had the forward engine room for his battle station and was awake most of the time. I would guess that he only slept 5 hours out of every 24 hours. He checked the two firerooms and engine rooms at all hours of the day and night and worried about the welfare of his men and the performance of his engines. He did not delegate authority well, but preferred to lead by example. He worked the same way as he advanced to Executive Officer and Commanding Officer. He knew how to perform our duties as well as we did. Once when we were underway, I had the lower-level watch and was working on a leak under the main condenser. Mr. Cochran came down to the lower level. When he didn't see me, I stopped work and called to him. In a second, he was in the bilge with me, checking my work and getting just as dirty as I was. He asked me many questions, crawled around with me to see the steam lines and valves, and then had me take my exam for machinist's mate second class. I passed with a grade of 3.40 without even studying for it. I still have my certificate now. It's signed by J. W. Rogers, Ensign E-VG, USNR, and our Executive Officer, Tom C. "Scratchass" Phifer, who later became a rear admiral.

As a ship, we were not ready to fight yet in 1942, but we were getting more shipshape every day. We had a fine competition going between the engine rooms and the firerooms. If the engine room got a signal for flank speed, we would answer it with reckless abandon and try to pull enough steam into the turbines to make the steam pressure go down in the boilers. After a while, it was hard to lower the pressure. They were learning to cut in extra burners with lightning speed. After about a week, if you were on the fantail when we went to flank speed, the stern would lower into the water and tilt like a speedboat at flank speed when we were making a port or starboard turn. Sometimes it seemed like the ship wanted to plane. In these ways, we were getting ready for battle; we found

N. Nav. 84
(Sept., 1929)

The United States of America

Navy Department & Bureau of Navigation

Navy Training Course Certificate

Emory Joseph Jernigan, #268 59 60, F1c   USN

having completed the Navy Training Course

Machinist's Mate Second Class

with a mark of ___3.40___, is awarded this certificate this ___18___

Day of ___February___, 19_43_ Notation of this effort has been made in

his service record.

J. W. Rogers.
J. W. ROGERS, E-VG   USNR

Ensign   U. S. Navy,
Division Officer.

Lieut. Commander U. S. Navy,
Commanding
U. S. S. SAUFLEY

J. C. PHIFER

The author showing promise for a successful naval career; passes his MM2 training course. Later events were to limit his advancement.

out that speed, maneuvering, shooting, and plenty of luck are what wins for you.

Our engine room had a cruising engine that saved fuel, a main engine for speed, and a backdown or reverse engine. The cruising engine worked with steam at 600°F. The main engine used saturated steam at 600°F or superheated steam at 800°F for high-speed running or battle conditions. Under these conditions, the fireroom had to cut in the superheaters, which were extremely hot and could burn the boiler tubes up in seconds. When we went to flank speed, the turbines would whine like banshees, and all the pumps and blowers would strain to their utmost. On a sharp turn, the engine and pumps would make a different noise as the ship leaned to one side. Then as we straightened up, it would change tune once more as if someone was conducting a big band. On a hard turn, the lights would dim and the men had to hold onto something. The big bolts and engine binding were put under much strain in each attack. The drive shaft bearings got hot at times under this all-out strain. Only one drive shaft bearing ever burned out. It's a credit to the builders that the ships lasted as many years as they did. We were all proud to serve on this fine fighting ship.

With the shakedown cruise completed, we took several East Coast cruises and then left Norfolk, Virginia, on November 9, 1942, with the destroyer *DeHaven* and cruiser *Columbus* for the Panama Canal. On the way to Panama, we had constant training with every division on board participating. I kept up with the rapid improvement in firing rounds-per-minute, but I knew we were slow in firing the 5-inch 38 main battery. Fifteen rounds-per-minute was our best at this point.

We arrived at the Panama Canal and started through on November 13, 1942. We entered the canal at Colon and anchored briefly at Lake Gatun, which is a freshwater lake. The lake and shoreline looked like God had painted a picture and was giving us a preview. As we moved up the canal through the Gaillard and Calebra cuts, the beauty shown in any direction took your breath away. The heat, however, was so oppressive we all breathed with our mouths open, the worst day I can remember. I guess it was because I was still used to the cold temperatures above the Arctic Circle in the North Atlantic area.

When we were in the canal locks, we saw soldiers on watch with anti-aircraft guns and people working to pump water in and out of the locks. Scratches on the concrete on each side of the locks were caused by the North Carolina-class battleships hitting the sides as they were pulled through the locks by the donkey engines. The battleships had only a few inches of clearance on each side, and the damaged concrete bore testimony to their passage. We were talking about what would happen if we had an air attack while we were in the locks. As we worked our way through to Balboa and the Pacific, everyone started to listen to the stories of the older sailors about Pearl Harbor and the Asiatic Fleet. They also listened closely to my North Atlantic tales about storms, icebergs, the beauty of the northern lights, the Arctic Circle, and the merchant seamen in PQ17 who were killed in the cold waters. It was a time to get to know one another as shipmates. We started to believe in one another and control the fear of the unknown hidden in every man's heart. In doing this, we all became as one within *Saufley*.

Once we cleared the canal, it was back to drill, day and night. We needed it badly. Our 5-inch 38 guns were now getting off 18 rounds about every 60 seconds, almost as good as the 5-inch 38 on *Washington*, which could get 22 rounds per minute. On *Washington*, there was a competition between the Marines and sailors over who could shoot the fastest. On *Saufley*, the contest was among gun mount numbers one, two, three, four, and five. The Gunnery Officer, Lieutenant John C. Bangert, was really pushing us to get out every shot we could. He was looking for speed and would settle for accuracy later.

After we had been at sea for three or four days heading for the South Pacific, I sat on the after life raft and timed the shooting from the number five gun mount. They were firing for speed and were getting around 19 shots per minute at a sleeve towed by a plane for anti-aircraft practice. They were beginning to get the speed, but they still needed more accuracy. They weren't hitting anywhere near the target and would have to improve in a hurry, for we were on our way to battle.

Soon we were out of range of the planes stationed in the Canal zone and didn't have towed sleeves any more. We practiced by having the number three mount fire a burst in the air. Then, all the other gun mounts would whirl and shoot at it. This tactic proved effective because it wasn't long before those shell bursts were bunching close together up in the sky. You could tell our success by the way the gunners walked and talked. Later, we were very proud of our fine gun crews.

We were as good then as any destroyer anywhere on any sea. Even the ammunition handlers below deck had a gleam in their eyes. Without them, it couldn't have happened. I have described the 5-inch 38 gun crews as a well-trained example because they were more readily observed, but everyone was working just as hard. The torpedo men couldn't shoot their torpedoes because of the cost. All they could do was shine and polish them and make sure they were in first-class condition. The only way you could judge them was by their work, and they were working very hard.

Bales of rags, cleaned as if they would be used in a hospital operating room, were used by every division on board. The engineers used the most. We would wipe up anything in sight, then polish all the metal and floor plates, the throttle board, the pumps, and the valve handles. Each man had his own station to keep clean; he would get mean as a junkyard dog if anyone got it dirty. Keeping your station clean was one duty in your blood if you were in *Saufley* and she was in you.

We sailed further into the Pacific Ocean day after day, and we soon realized its immensity. On November 17, 1942, we approached and crossed over the equator. Even though it was wartime, we observed all the great traditions connected to crossing this line. Pollywogs, as they were called, were people who had never crossed the equator. On the day of crossing, you could do anything you wanted to a pollywog. Lieutenant Commander Tom Phifer seemed to enjoy this trip across the equator more than anyone else. I heard a lot of the men say that Phifer was the meanest man on the ship. He had a very active part in the procedure. First, he had all the regular Navy men who hadn't crossed over run through and then start helping with the initiation of the others. They were a little easier on us than the boots because they didn't want a revolt. They figured if the boots revolted, some of us would lead them.

This is how Phifer observed crossing the equator. For the initiation, the slop chutes were filled with slop and water. The canvas targets usually towed by planes were filled with filth (fuel oil, oatmeal, cereal, and a few eggs). Men who had never crossed went through these on their hands and knees, got their butts beat, were shocked with electricity, and then had to kiss "the Royal Baby's butt." The "Royal Baby" was Machinist's Mate William E. LeBlanc. His belly, which hung over fairly good, was painted with mustard and all kinds of grease, making it look like a man's ass that had never been washed. He had on a pair of skivvy shorts like you wear in the Navy. His gun was showing so that when a boot come out of the canvas, he didn't know what he had to kiss. They were glad when they could kiss the "Royal Baby's butt."

Shortly after we reached the Solomons, Lieutenant Commander Phifer was transferred to a new command as captain of a destroyer escort. The ship transferring him to his new command was sunk, and the ship that picked him up was the ship Lieutenant Commander Phifer was to command. When he saw it, he yelled, "That's my ship, that's my ship."

All this time Commander Brown was watching over the safety of the $12-million ship he had signed for back in Brooklyn and the 320 sailors in his care. Doggone if he was going to let anything happen to us. Our cooks and bakers were serving good chow prepared from less than adequate supplies. At times in the near future, we would have to resort to sea rations and hardtack without any cigarettes. Cooks were only as good as the food supply, but the bakers were a head taller than anyone.

They handed out something special most of the time. We had the very best of bread, cakes, and doughnuts at all times but not in excess since they couldn't cook too much at a time.

Mess cooking or cook's helper was a dirty job that most people tried to avoid. You had to get up early and work until late at night washing pots, trays, and silverware; peeling Irish potatoes (if we had them); and making coffee and drinks. Serving on the chow line wasn't easy either. You had to put the proper amount on each man's tray, making sure to treat everyone equally. Each man wanted more of what he liked and would fuss with the mess cook. At the same time, the cook was watching to make sure everyone got the same ration. Mess cooks were often in fights with disgruntled sailors who felt slighted. As the supply line grew longer and the number of ships and troops increased many times in size, our food supply dwindled. To make the best use of the available cargo space, the shift was made to instant tea and lemonade. Meat, such as Spam, was shipped in cans to eliminate the need for refrigeration. Milk was all powdered; you added water and tried to drink it! All these products were new and not as good as they are now, but while we complained, the enemy had much less to eat than we did.

We arrived at New Caledonia, a French possession, on December 2, 1942, and went under command of the Commander South Pacific area. Six days later, we arrived at Lunga Point, Guadalcanal, escorting troop ships. I found myself thinking of the old western movies. Just like the old cowboys and Indians circled the wagons and fought, we circled around the troop ships when there was an air alert.

After 29 days of sailing, we had reached the battlefield. The enemy was an unknown to us. Some of us had never seen a Japanese or known one as a person. He was known from his own propaganda as mean and cruel. From the way he fought in China, we knew that he gave no quarter. He had wrecked our fleet in Pearl Harbor in a surprise attack, and he had kicked our butts here in the South Pacific before *Saufley* arrived. The waters around Guadalcanal had run red with our Navy and

Marine blood. Over the next 20 months, we learned to fight him. We came to believe he was slime, like wet manure in a cow pen not worthy of life. We wanted to send him, creepy and crawly, to hell any way we could; seeing dead Japanese in the water was like making love to a beautiful girl. We learned that no quarter in battle can work both ways. Time and distance plus loneliness make a tasteless soup, hard to stomach for long periods of time, and ours was a long, long time. We learned that each island in the Solomons chain was one lone battle. We had sharp, deadly fights at sea while the Marines and Army landed with no thought of mobility in battle. It was kill or be killed. The Japanese had to learn to die. They did.

⚓ 5 ⚓

UNDER THE SOUTHERN CROSS

DECEMBER 1942 – MARCH 1943

Initially assigned to escort reinforcements from Espiritu Santo to Lunga Point, Saufley *soon undertook antishipping sweeps in the waters north and west of Guadalcanal and conducted shore bombardment missions against enemy positions on the island. During the Japanese evacuation of Guadalcanal in late January and early February 1943,* Saufley *operated with Task Force 11. On 19 February, she sailed for Lunga Roads to join with other units staging for Operation "Cleanslate", the occupation of the Russells.*

During that operation, Saufley *transported troops, towed landing craft to the target islands, and provided shore bombardment in support of the troops as they landed on Pavuvu and Banika islands on the 21st. From these islands, planes would be able to cover operations against Rendova.*

—from The Dictionary of American Naval Fighting Ships

In the confined area around Savo Island, the Allies had met the enemy, won, lost, cried, and died in five crucial battles: Battle of Savo, August 9, 1942; Battle of Cape Esperance, October 11, 1942; Battle of Guadalcanal, November 13, 1942; Battle of Guadalcanal, November 14 and 15, 1942; and the Battle of Tassafaronga, November 30, 1942. Both Japanese and American losses were heavy from battleships to destroyers and from admirals to seamen. Even months after the battles, we could still see oil leaking to the surface and bits and pieces of surfaced evidence of death. The five Sullivan brothers died aboard the cruiser *Juneau*, on November 13, 1942 following a night action off Guadalcanal. A new destroyer was named for them. I can think of no spot on earth or sea more closely associated with heroes than Guadalcanal, the Island of Death and Indispensable Straight. The people had good reason to demand and get an explanation of how in the hell these losses had occurred. I knew we had plenty to fight with because I had seen our material on the way to Russia and England. But here we were almost forgotten for we were fighting with no backup of supplies or ships.

On December 8, 1942, after these terrible losses, we men of *Saufley* made the scene. One of the first things we saw on arriving at Tulagi Harbor was Admiral Halsey's sign, which said, "Kill Japs, Kill Japs, Kill the Yellow Bastards. If you do your job, you will kill the sons of bitches." The sign was at least 40 feet by 60 feet; we could read it from anywhere in the anchorage.

Daylight belonged to us but the night belonged to the Japanese. In addition to their night-fighting capability, they had land-based planes and great harbors at Empress Augusta Bay, Bougainville, and Rabaul. In my mind's eye, I can still see the long, low coast of Guadalcanal with bombed-out ships along the beach. I can still remember the feeling of utter loss that hits you when you sail over the many good men and American ships now permanently based at the bottom of Ironbottom Sound. The longer we were based at Tulagi, the more we came to realize the horror of Indispensable Straight, now known as Ironbottom Sound.

One of the first things we had to do was escort heavy cruiser *Minneapolis* out of the battle zone and back to Espirito Santo in the New Hebrides Islands group. It was sad duty. Its bow had been blown away in a quick, savage fight on November 30, 1942, with eight Japanese destroyers that had kicked the daylights out of our Task Force 67. When we first saw *Minneapolis*, she had no bow and her main propulsion was badly damaged. She was tied to trees ashore and camouflaged by cut trees placed on the deck and in the rigging. Repair crews worked like ants to get her ready to head back for repairs. Our job was to guard her in the harbor and escort her back to Espirito Santo. We did this at a speed of 4 knots for 600 miles. One cruiser and one destroyer, six days of constant movement for us, looking for planes and submarines. *Minneapolis* could manage only a 4-knot speed, and we cursed the fact that we were the only escort destroyer. When we reached the anchorage, we had to tie up to *Minneapolis* like a tug and deliver the ship right up to the repair ship. The crew was really grateful for our part in delivering them to semi-safety; we were sad to see them leave when they were needed most. The battle was positive proof that our new ships coming online with new, hastily trained men had much to learn in a hurry.

We arrived in the war zone with no radar and no proximity fuses for anti-aircraft. Our torpedoes were not good. While some worked, most of them didn't. We shot our first plane down at night from five miles out right after our radar was in operation. In daylight raids, we could look at dogfights between our planes and the Japanese and see our pilots start to win. With our new planes hitting the Japanese from above at high speed, the men were getting over the first shock of mortal combat and starting to regain self-respect. We needed good radar, flashless powder, proximity fuses, better torpedoes, and senior officers who were not tentative. I mean strike first and follow through. Task Force 67 had lost some 400 men in this fight, but we were learning.

December 25, 1942, was not a day like all others. We were all adjusting to death, each in his own fashion. Some men prayed and were calm and secure in their own religious beliefs. Others were fighting with their own thoughts; some never completely adjusted. We had to go to larger ships to worship. We missed our religion at Christmas time most of all. A few Christmas presents arrived, but care packages were in short supply and missed very much. Everyone laughed and talked of home and the differences in the night stars, moon, and weather. Once again, many tears wet Navy pillows on a Christmas night.

Our cooks and bakers did a great job providing the typical Christmas dinner. They were good, but how can a Navy cook or baker compare to your own Mom on this most holy of days? They couldn't. I missed the evening star most of all. Christmas mail from a girlfriend or wife was hard to take, yet just as necessary as grits and eggs at a breakfast in the deep South.

The rest of December we operated with a cruiser task group and as a screening ship for troop transports to Guadalcanal. On January 2 or 3, 1943, we bombarded enemy positions at Kokumbona and continued screening troopships for the Guadalcanal area until January 17. Then, from January 18 until February 11, we had gunnery practice off the island of New Caledonia.

Our sister ship, *DeHaven*, was sunk close to Savo in a bad little fight. She was our sister ship in line of construction and DD number. *DeHaven* was a Fletcher-class ship commissioned September 21, 1942, and had left Norfolk, Virginia, in company with *Saufley*. *DeHaven* was sunk 133 days after her commissioning on February 1, 1943. Japanese planes surprised *DeHaven* as she was escorting three landing craft about two miles south of Savo Island. Six Vals came in to attack *DeHaven* and went right through her anti-aircraft fire. Three bombs hit, and there were some near misses. I talked with some of the survivors later. They said they were below decks and, by the time they fought their way up through the fires, she was going down by her bow. She was the fifteenth destroyer lost at Guadalcanal. One hundred and sixty seven men died in just a few flicks of time. Only four of the ship's officers survived and one of them was wounded badly. The Captain died when a bomb hit his ship.

Destroyer *Nicholas*, in the meantime, had stood off an attack by eight Vals. She had two men killed and sustained damage to her steering gear. The landing craft had shot down one of the attacking planes. *Saufley* survived many attacks. To survive, you had to have luck as well as the men who would stick to their guns until the enemy planes hit them. Ours would. You had to have speed and deceptive moves, but most of all, you had to have a Captain who was not afraid to con the ship. Ours wasn't. We answered his commands and survived as a unit. We also shot at unidentified planes. It was the only way.

February 19, 1943, we landed Company E of the 169th Infantry on Guadalcanal as relief for the Marines. There were minor air attacks in progress during the landing. The enemy was after any shipping in the Guadalcanal area, which was now a staging area for our nightly runs up the "Slot." These attacks came day or night with as few as one or as many as 75 to 100 planes. Staff Sergeant Walter L. Gulledge from Monroe, North Carolina, was one of the soldiers we landed. After the February 19 landing, Gulledge's next trip under escort of *Saufley* was to New Georgia Island as a sergeant of a heavy machine gun unit where he was wounded in battle. Three of his fellow soldiers were killed in this fight. The next time *Saufley* crossed Gulledge's path was at Lingayen Gulf in the Philippine Islands. We screened for this largely unopposed landing. During Gulledge's service in the Pacific, he made three major landings. His unit was cited three different times in battle. At the end of the fighting, there were only three left of the original Company E soldiers who had been landed at Guadalcanal. Gulledge was one.

We went back to Guadalcanal on February 20th. We made nine trips to the Russell Island landings, including the original landing. We were jack-of-all-trades for this operation: transporting the troops, covering vessel, and acting as a tugboat towing landing craft to the landing site. I knew one of the troops from former duty in Philadelphia and let him sleep on my bunk. I slept topside to avoid the heat and kept my clean clothes folded on my bunk. In a few days, I had one of the damnedest doses of crabs in the South Pacific as a reward for my generosity.

Not one of the troops that I saw gave any evidence of fear when landing on the beach, but many of them were deathly afraid to be aboard ship around all the explosives that we carried, both theirs on deck and ours in the magazines below deck. It was only with great reluctance that some of them went below for chow. Most of the men were new to the service and had not served aboard ship, unlike many of the fleet Marines, who had sailed in peacetime. I guess if we had been strafed or bombed, we would have left with a big bang. The fight against planes and submarines was continuous; we were attacked by planes at all times of the day and night.

We looked like a duck with little ones following as we sailed along with our cluttered decks, towing LCVPs (landing craft vehicle personnel) behind us. The tows kept us at speeds of 9 or 10 knots, or they would swing back and forth. They were on lines at 500, 600, or 700-foot intervals loaded with crew and supplies. We carried everything from ammunition to "C" rations on deck and a full load of troops all over the main deck, many of them seasick and all of them asking questions. We were at Modified General Quarters or General Quarters at all times. Our air cover was beefed up in case of an air attack. During this operation, *Saufley* made nine trips from Guadalcanal to the landing site at Russell Island.

We spent the last days of March 1943 alongside USS *Rigel*, a destroyer tender, at Havana Harbor, New Hebrides. April, May, and June were spent exercising with the fleet and on escort duty. These group exercises were necessary for forming battle groups and for gunnery practice, formation sailing, anti-aircraft defense, spotting and identifying aircraft, and fueling at sea. We had one week's availability alongside USS *Dobbin* in Sydney, Australia, in early May.

Our boiler tubes were burned up when the bridge called for extra steam temperatures from 600°F to 800°F. Commander Cochran had requested Captain Brown to notify him personally before he ordered the superheater lit. Captain Brown forgot, and the tubes were melted down by an inexperienced crew who were not used to superheaters. Captain Brown assumed complete responsibility and informed the admiral through Commodore Burke. He also relieved the chief water tender of any responsibility.

We couldn't keep up with the fleet, but Admiral Halsey had given orders that no fighting ship was to leave the area under his command. Commodore Burke took it upon himself to send us to Sydney for repair. When he was called on the mat, he told Admiral Halsey he had sent us to Sydney for whiskey. Captain Brown bought some and put it in his footlocker. Halsey grinned and let Burke get by with it. Because of this Sydney trip, we were known as the "Whiskey Ship." This story appeared later in *Reader's Digest*; it was sent in by Admiral Burke, who was then Chief of Naval Operations.

It seemed that both Admiral Halsey and Commodore Burke had more of a weakness for hard-drinking hell-raisers than other Naval officers at the time. The hard-drinking hell-raisers had a soft spot in their hearts for Halsey and Burke. On the other hand, the real fighting officers and enlisted men had no place in their hearts for prima donnas.

Paul DeRosa was Italian and figured he was good-looking. He was short, with a large jaw and typical Italian face. His black, curly hair was the kind girls really liked, and he was like a peacock about it. Pop Mowrey cut our hair. He would bring his tools topside and anyone could use them. If Pop wasn't close by, we would clip each other's hair. Most of us had boot camp haircuts anyway, so when Paul asked me to cut his hair, I did. He sat on Pop's seat, and I started at the back of his neck, cutting straight up. I had cut three or four inches when Paul realized what I was doing to him. He was the maddest Roman I ever came in contact with. Paul wanted to fight and I said OK, but he never hit me and finally walked away. I don't know who finished his hair for him. He never asked me to cut it again.

While we were in Sydney for repairs and liberty, Paul went ashore. When we were at sea again, he came down to the lower level and presented arms to me. With tears in his eyes he asked, "Jernigan, have I gotta clap? Have I gotta clap?" I laughed and said, "Paul, if you have to ask me, you sure have! Go and see Frederick Wilhelm." He left crying and the shanker mechanic had another customer.

Arriving in Sydney, we were greeted by a skyline of excessive beauty with a bridge that took your breath away. Friendly Aussies were on the dock to greet us with a big freezer full of free ice cream that never ran out. At breakfast, we had steak and eggs, which fast became a habit for many of us. There were bread puddings, egg puddings, and pies of all kinds—including blood pie and liver pudding. I had eaten them before at Grandmother McAlpin's, who made all kinds of foods from the old country including barley soup for winter colds.

We were in Sydney for seven days. It was a great liberty port. All the people there realized that we were fighting for the life of their country and the cold thought of defeat was on everyone's mind. They had good Scotch whiskey, and their beer, called Tasmanian beer, was strong.

Australia had girls, too, of all kinds—blonde, brunette, redheads, pretty, not-so-pretty, pregnant, not-so-pregnant, and not-at-all pregnant—waiting for their Yank, or any Yank at all, to come down the dock. The women were great and wanted a man in their lives. The Australian veterans of the 7th and 9th Divisions returning from Tobruk and the African fighting resented us though. Many fine fights occurred. Some won and some lost, but fun was had by all. Many of our men married Australian women. Some returned to Australia after the war; others took their brides home to the states. As much as we loved Sydney, after seven days we had to leave. The repairs were finished, and we had to return to the war.

Back at sea on a clear night and calm sea, it was like a great looking glass. The moon would form a golden pathway that seemed to go on forever in a long line clear to the far horizon. The other end of the pathway wound up right at your feet, just as if God had decided to anoint you with moondust. The flying fish could be seen in the moonlight, just as Rudyard Kipling had described them in his poem *Road to Mandalay*. The stars were the brightest and clearest you could imagine. The Milky Way and the Southern Cross had a beauty not equalled anywhere else in this universe of ours. Small wonder that the Marines took the Southern Cross as a shoulder patch.

Members of the crew take time out for a photo session. Pictured above from top left, are: F1c Omolecki, MM2 Einhorn, WT1 Coffman, WT3 Curry, EM3 Duffy, EM2 Vordick. Note censored radar screen.   PHOTO, WILLIS NORMAN

Top photo, from top left, are: QM3 Warner, COX Dace, S1c Delong, QM3 Zender, Unidentified sailor, unidentified sailor.

Lower photo, from top left, are: RM3 Dienes, S1c Wilson, RM3 Covert, RM3 Grant, RM3 Dupere, RM3 Duffy, RM2 Benoit.

PHOTO, WILLIS NORMAN

At night as we steamed along, we left a broad trail of glowing lights in the water behind us where the propellers disturbed the water. Small sea creatures in the water caused this trail of light behind the ship, and I always wondered if an enemy pilot could see it and follow us.

These same opiates of tropical beauty could become obscene and hateful if you were on a night run up the "Slot." In the early days, we were outnumbered and outgunned. The Japanese had started the battle in the South Pacific with a back-breaking defeat for us by sinking five destroyers, three cruisers, and an aircraft carrier in the first nine weeks. They were far superior to us in all types of ships. The Japanese fleet in the South Pacific possessed 5 aircraft carriers, 5 battleships, 14 cruisers, and 44 destroyers. For our part, we had 2 carriers, 2 battleships, 9 cruisers, and 24 destroyers. The equation worked out to 68 Japanese ships against 37 U.S. ships. Later, to cap that off, we lost another aircraft carrier, two cruisers, and eight destroyers. Our greatest asset at the time was the Fletcher-class destroyer coming into the crucible together with Admiral Halsey and his fighting spirit.

One sight that impressed everyone was the destruction of a freighter, SS *John Penn*, in 1943. We were at Modified General Quarters about nine miles away at the time. I was sitting on the fantail on a big life raft talking to one of the 20-mm gun crewmen when suddenly everyone began pointing at Guadalcanal. When I turned around, all kinds of fireworks were in the air and the boom of explosives was coming toward us in waves. *John Penn* had been unloading cargo and must have had lots of ammunition on board. The explosions took the shape of a water fountain spraying up into the air, dissipating in force with smoke, which was mostly white with some dark black. I got a cold, clammy feeling watching it and wondered how many people had been killed. I kept looking for a plane that I couldn't see and hating the enemy more with each passing moment.

⚓ 6 ⚓

DEATH AND THE FLUTTER-WILLIES
(and Remember These Things)

MARCH 1943 – JULY 1943

In March, Saufley *resumed escort and antisubmarine duties in the southern Solomons—New Caldeonia—New Hebrides area. Following an abbreviated availability at Sydney, Australia, she returned to Noumea and resumed escort work until the end of June. On the 30th, as Allied forces moved toward Rendova,* Saufley *bombarded Japanese shore installations there.*
        —*from* The Dictionary of American Naval Fighting Ships

T he Solomon Islands had a smell like wild flowers, yet death's smell was always in the air in 1943. When the moon was out, the floral smell reminded you of a special girl back home. The Southern Cross was an eternal promise standing in the sky looking down at you. The romantic names like San Cristobal, Guadalcanal, Tassafaronga, Savo, Henderson Field, Tenaru River, Lunga Point, Cape Esperance, Sea Lark Channel, Ironbottom Sound, the Slot, Purvis Bay, Tulagi, Russell Island, Munda, Vella, New Georgia, Vella Gulf, Vella Lavella, Kolombangara, Treasury Island, Shortland Island, Bougainville, Empress Augusta Bay, Buka, Blackett Straight, Green Island, Cape St. George, and Rabaul all remain in a veteran's memory if he spent time there. These islands were looked at and enjoyed for their beauty and, at the same time, they were feared for the death and destruction that was in them at the time, and then stored in memories forever.

Allen Levinson, Joe Tannenbaum, Mickey Samuels, and I had just finished working out one day and rushed to the chow line before it closed. We found that everyone was getting two fried oysters. I had a fit about just getting two oysters and said I'd give $1.00 each for more of them. I didn't know Jewish boys didn't eat oysters. With that one fast offer, I got to pay $6.00 for what my friends had intended to give me. Everyone laughed at me when they found out what my big mouth had cost me.

Everyone had a sheath knife on his belt. In case we were sunk, it was our only defense against sharks. Since we had no arms of any kind, it was an all-purpose weapon. We had plenty of rifles on board and, when we were close to Japanese on the beach, we could check one out to shoot at them, which many of us did. I had a Marine K-bar knife, but the men made many beautiful knives by hand with heavy blades and leather handles. Others used Plexiglas from the cockpit covers of fighter planes for handles. Getting a piece of a Japanese fighter plane's Plexiglas was considered good luck.

I remember the time a lone Japanese plane pulled a sneak raid when we were anchored at Tulagi and proceeded to drop a bomb close enough to shake us up real good. A few of us were still eating chow. One of the new men, just aboard ship and just out of boot camp, was across the table from me. He hopped up from the bench in a flash, stepped to the tabletop in one fast, fluid motion, and rammed his head into an overhead line covered with lagging. It didn't break the skin on his head, but he fell back onto the table in the trays of chow, broke wind, rolled off the table, and was gone in a flash. This event was just one of the merry little things that made life bearable at sea in time of war.

Japanese Admiral Yamamoto was also shot down and killed by Army fighter planes when he came for an inspection trip to Bougainville. With advance intelligence, three P38 Lightnings

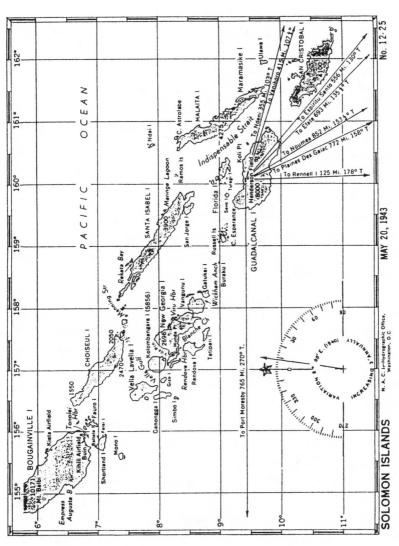

Hydrographic Office air chart of the Solomon Islands, May 1943.

N.A.C.I. HYDROGRAPHIC OFFICE   NATIONAL ARCHIVES

lay in wait for him and blew him out of the sky. We all knew through Navy scuttlebutt that we were supposed to have had his code. I can't see why the Japanese never figured it out.

George Duffy worked in the radio shack and was a good source of scuttlebutt, some of it true. George had a playful streak and would invent information at times that would stand your hair on end. Chief McAdams was a master dispenser of good scuttlebutt. Jim Fagan would get a good crowd and drop some pure nuggets that you had better believe, but not trust. "Doc" Fore was most convincing and casual enough to be listened to. Chief Curley was convincing and true most of the time. Lieutenant Michie was always as reliable as the story of Santa Claus at Christmas. When you put it all together, you had all the information contained in *The New York Times* in the best tradition of good Navy scuttlebutt.

Wynt Rogers, new to the Navy and nearly 36 years old, was on watch in the after fireroom with Bob Cromie, who was about 19 years old. Cromie was the water tender on watch; Wynt hated him for being young, lazy, and in charge. Cromie spent a large part of each watch lying between the boilers on the deck plates with a rolled-up shirt for a pillow. From this vantage point, he could see all the gauges on both boilers, the fireman on watch, and the ladder that old Chief Knight used to come down to the fireroom. (Knight spent much time sitting topside in the cooler air.) Wynt had become so frustrated with Cromie that he requested a transfer to the forward engine room to strike for machinist's mate, which Lieutenant Rogers, our Engineering Officer, had approved. One night when everything seemed normal, Cromie suddenly leaped up and flew around like crazy, turning valves off and on, jumping over steam lines, and yelling to the other men. The pumps had lost suction, and no one had noticed it quick enough to react. Wynt had a new respect for Bob after that (and a transfer to the forward engine room, which he really didn't want).

Jim Fagan was the best friend I ever had. We met in the brig at Pier 92. I don't know why he was there, but we were happy when we left together for *Saufley*. We split Captain

Brown's $5.00 loan on a visit to Sand Street. Fagan had been a railroader in real life and wore a red bandanna around his neck while at sea. He was a good sailor from the first day and had all the instincts of a fighting man. Jim was a typical Columbus, Ohio, Irishman. Sometimes he would start to dance and sing Irish tunes. Once in Clearwater, Florida, at least 20 people followed us out of one restaurant, right down the street, and into another restaurant while singing along with Jim. He was short, stout, and strong with a scarred, ugly face, yet he reminded me of one of the wee folk of Irish lore who danced in the moonlight and could only be seen by the blessed. People just loved him. It was a wonder to see him in a fight; he never threw the first punch but always threw a counterpunch that usually ended the fight very quickly. In Columbus, he had been a sparring mate for Fritzie Zivic when Zivic was a middleweight fighter.

We had three men aboard that needed descriptively correct names. When Fagan renamed them, the names stuck. They all worked in the firerooms. Two of them had great big dingdongs. Since one was a big man and one was smaller, they became "Big Bull" and "Little Bull." The third man had big breasts, so he became "Bubbles."

While operating out of Tulagi Harbor, Wynt decided to make some fudge. He was working in the after fireroom when Bob Cromie came on watch. Wynt and Little Bull had the George Abner Stoneham coffeepot full of fudge, and it was boiling away. After a few minutes, Bob told them to hurry up and finish so he could have some coffee. Thirty minutes later, the fudge was still hot and liquid. Bob told them to put it under the blower, which was going full blast. When the air hit, that hot, brown liquid was blown all over the small fireroom and partially up the ladder just as Chief Knight came down for a quick inspection. He took one look around and left saying, "Clean this damn place up," and they did. Wynt never tried making fudge again.

Alan Levinson was a true body-builder and trying to max out with all he could lift. One day he went to the forward engine room to the labyrinth packing on the forward main bearing of the engine and took half-pound weights off the counterbalance where steam was used to keep air pressure from getting to the engine chamber, which would cause us to lose vacuum and speed. True to form, he forgot and left the weights topside instead of putting them back where they belonged. When we got up steam late that afternoon and went on a run up the "Slot," our vacuum was at 25 inches instead of the 29 inches or 30 inches it should have been. All the engineers were going crazy hunting the air leak, for we truly needed more speed. The after engine room was turning up more revolutions than we were and was forced to slow down to match our slowed engine. After an hour or so, I thought about the weights, excused myself to go to the head, and returned with them in my pocket. After I slipped them back in place, everyone went crazy trying to figure what had happened. I had to keep it to myself for the chief would have had Alan's hide! Chief Curley kept asking me what I had done, thinking it was another one of my tricks he knew about, such as making the gauge on the evaporators show salty water.

When we received a shipment of new boots, it was hard not only on them but also on the older sailors. First of all, the boots were in shock at the transition from civilian to military life in a war zone. We had to train them quickly and send them back to man new construction. I can still see the shock on an 18-year-old face when we gave him hell for the smallest mistake.

Donald "Grom" Addison was a machinist's mate first class from the old Asiatic Fleet with blond hair and eyes so blue they looked weak. I think the nickname referred to a grommet, which was a hole punched in a piece of canvas and reinforced around the edges. He would sit and stare at the sea for long periods of time, not talking to anyone. It would disturb the men just arrived from the states. We told them to watch him when they were in the washroom and, if they were taking a shower and dropped the soap, never to stoop over and pick it up for he would be after them in a second. Poor old Grom never

The author with a few weight-lifting friends. Pictured from top left are: MM3 Allan Levinson, MM2 Joseph Denuptiis, the author; YN1 Bertrand Curtin, YN3 Milton Samuels, and MaM3 Edward Duffy.

PHOTO, WILLIS NORMAN

figured out why the new men would get out of the showers like they were answering a call to General Quarters when he came in. After a few months, they would spread the tale to new arrivals.

One of the things that I missed most at sea was a walk in the woods. My feet did not touch the earth from December 8, 1942, until May 23, 1943, which was a long time to be cooped up with 300 other people, all of whom were in the same shape. For relaxation, we played backgammon, checkers, and cards; worked out with the weights; boxed; jumped rope; ran around the deck; and punched a timing bag. We made our own weights and read books. The magazines were sometimes three months old. The ones we liked best were *Time*, *Newsweek*, *Look*, *Life*, *Reader's Digest*, and *The Saturday Evening Post*. Books were like hen's teeth: hard to find. We could not have a radio, so the best way to become informed was to read. I never once heard Tokyo Rose. Women were a lot scarcer than books, but we had pinups all over the ship. One of Esther Williams was on the throttle board in the forward engine room.

Anytime we anchored at an island with recreational facilities, we played baseball. Mr. Rogers managed our baseball team. He was our Engineering Officer and a good man. When I asked to play, he said no because Fagan was the catcher. All I wanted to do was to get ashore and get drunk, he said. I hated Rogers for that because he had read my mind. When we left the ship after the war, I refused to shake his hand. It hurt him a lot, and I have always been ashamed of what I did. Some of the others also refused. I will apologize to him if I see him in this life. After death, it won't matter.

One time we were at sea, sailing at a speed of at least 10 knots into waves of 2 feet or 3 feet. A. N. Mote and W. M. Norman were playing chess. Norman sat cross-legged on the deck right on top of the ship's expansion joint, which would move very smartly when we hit a large wave on rough seas. Everything was smooth and Norman was on the verge of a brilliant move, when we hit a wave of 5 feet or 6 feet. The moving joint caught his butt and pinched it so hard he thought it was cutting him in half. His reaction really startled Motes, who was at least five feet away, with a shocked look on his face when the joint turned loose. He thought Norman had lost his mind and was cussing him! He also wondered why Norman upset the chessboard.

Checkers was a popular game. Fagan, Huffine, some other men, and I were very good at it. Then, a seaman from Tennessee named Goodlett came aboard with a new draft of boots. He would hum and sing hillbilly music as he played checkers. We played him separately and as a group, but we never had a chance! He had a real killer instinct. We never came close to beating him, and we were all real poor losers.

When we were going to anchor for a night, we would hear the word passed, "Set the anchor watch." All hands would scramble with seaman rushing right and left checking their anchor chains and making certain everything had been done to perfection. After all hands reported, it was time to drop anchor with the anchor chain making much noise and the anchor hitting the water. When the anchor hit bottom, both engines would reverse and back down to set the flukes on the anchor so we wouldn't drift.

If the captain was going ashore, his gig would be lowered into the water, the motor whaleboat would be lowered, the firerooms and engine rooms would set cold iron watch, and the shipmates would stand around in small groups telling the latest scuttlebutt. If we were in a safe place, movies might be shown. You can't imagine what a relief it was to anchor and get a rest from being underway and battle-ready. We only did this on rare occasions, but they are still fresh in my mind.

A. C. Newby of McMinnville, Tennessee, was a good shipmate from the old four-piper fleet. He was hooked on anchor pools. If we were going to anchor some place, he would cut sixty pieces of paper with all the minutes of the hour and sell chances to shipmates for $1.00. The winner had the same time as written in the logbook. Newby always took his cut.

At times, we would pull in to some anchorage and, instead of anchoring, we would tie up to another destroyer. This allowed two destroyers to anchor in the same area that only one would normally use. Since we would move with the tide on these occasions, a walkway was always placed between the ships. We could visit each other and have boxing matches, chess games, checkers, and acey deucy. We could also gamble or swap movies. The officers would visit and the captains would exchange battle tactics and get to know each other. Sometimes when the squadron commander would come aboard, a good and restful time would be had by all. These visits always resulted in better coordination of efforts.

When we were going to tie up to a larger ship, such as an oil tanker or supply ship, we would go in at a slight angle, bow first, and get close enough to cast a light line to the mother ship. The heavy line would be tied to this, and the mother ship's seaman would make it fast. If we were lucky, we could back down when the lines were doubled up and swing right into place next to the mother ship or dock. Then we could take on oil or supplies, mail, and ammunition, making ready to go to sea again.

At sea with a fast task group or on a long convoy with an invasion group, we had to take on fuel from larger warships, such as a tanker, cruiser, battleship, or, at times, an aircraft carrier. We would pull up beside the mother ship and match its speed while maintaining a clear distance. Small lines would be shot from ship to ship with larger lines attached. A larger line was then used to pull the fuel line into position between the two ships. The fuel lines were in approximate 20-foot-long sections connected together. The fuel line was a six or eight-inch diameter line. Fuel was then pumped under pressure into our tanks.

At this time of taking on fuel, we were all in extreme danger. If we drifted apart, the line could separate. If we went too close, we could have a collision since the ship could be moved easily by wave action. Sometimes, water would be knee-deep on the fantail, allowing sailors to go overboard in a second. It was a trying time, to say the least, for if an attack came we had to cut and run.

Three classic sailors take a topside break from below deck. Pictured from left are: EM2 Willis Norman, who took many of the photos in this book, EM1 Athel Mote, and EM3 Elmer Duffy.   PHOTO, ORVILLE ELLIOTT

Often, other operations were in process while we were taking on fuel. We also transferred food, men, and medical supplies on another line high in the rigging in an operation much like a ski lift. If we took a roll toward each other at the same time, someone took a dunking; or if we rolled apart at the same time, the line could separate. The passengers being transferred could be wounded, sick, or high-ranking officers. The captain was always on the bridge or flying bridge, chewing his nails and cutting thin washers, since he was totally responsible. Commander Cochran was extremely good at this job.

Saufley was a left-handed ship. We took on stores, bombarded, and ran to General Quarter down the port side. If we went into a hard turn in battle, nine out of ten times it was to the port side. I don't know if it was the way the ship was built or if it was the captain. It could have been Captain Cochran because, when we got Commander Silk, he changed everything, even our morale. I distinctly remember the LCVPs at Corregidor pulled up to the starboard side for medical help with the wounded and dead even though we were anchored and firing over the starboard side. Both the LCVP and the wounded were on the side close to the beach and in much greater danger than if *Saufley* had been between them and the Japanese.

Sometimes destroyers would take a fighter pilot on board and head up the "Slot." The pilot would act as a fighter director for the planes operating in this area. Major Joe Foss and a pilot named John Smith had been running neck and neck on kills until Mr. Smith was shot down. Smith became our fighter/director for the run up the "Slot." I have never seen anyone with eyes like his. The man was rather tall and thin, and his eyes were never still. Although a bird of prey has to move his head for his eyes to see, Mr. Smith could keep his head still and his eyes would move like the hawk or eagle moves his head. In the 30 minutes or more that I observed him, his eyes moved up, down, and sideways. You knew he could see everything at once and wondered how anyone had ever shot him down. On the surface, he was calm as could be, but I felt that he was a great bundle of nerves ready to explode at any moment. I don't know where he went or what he did after that, but his eyes were the most remarkable I have ever seen. He was an ace; you could tell it.

We had some musicians on board. O. R. Elliott played a guitar and sang. Clement Helminiak played the accordion. On many afternoons they would go to the fantail to play and sing. We would have great fun until afternoon General Quarters called us to our battle stations. I can still see our shipmates performing for us, and I still get a warm feeling for the veteran fighters I served with.

We worked with the landing force Marines and Army so often we were called General Patches' Bougainville Navy. We landed, screened, and covered for the landing parties. We were their anti-aircraft ship, using up 5-inch 38 shells by the thousands. Our gun barrels were often red hot. Once the gun bloomers on the number 5 gun caught fire; they were supposed to be fireproof! We must have saved thousands of our Marines and soldiers' lives while we scattered Japanese flesh all over the landscape. I would venture to say we killed thousands of enemy troops in the Pacific War.

Sometimes when I came from my battle station in the engine room, cork and cordite smell was everywhere and empty shell cases were all about. When we had a chance, we saved the cases and stacked them like cordwood on deck for return to the ammunition ship when we took on more ammunition. Below decks, this type of action made you sweat; it didn't matter who you were or what your rating or rank was.

Many times we could look up and see the great air battles as they were fought in the big sky above us. The battles included 150 or more planes involved in a 600-mile-long battlefield. Sometimes we had to hunt for pilots who were shot down. They were hard to find. The life rafts were yellow and so small that a man's head and feet would project on either side. Thirty or more lookouts were posted all over the ship. Everyone wanted to find the downed flyer for two reasons: first, he was one of us and second, we always got ice cream when we delivered him safely to a larger ship.

Valiant efforts were made by men on the Japanese destroyers to land supplies. The supplies were supposed to float in on
the tide in steel drums chained together. At daylight the American destroyer and PT men deep-sixed the steel drums with
20-mm, 40-mm, and 5-inch 38s. Finally the "Tokyo Express,"
a group of Japanese destroyers, rushed in and retrieved all the
remaining Japanese soldiers and hauled them back up the
"Slot." This was a remarkable feat since no one knew what
had happened until the U.S. forces moved in to destroy them
and found out that the Japanese were gone.

One morning when we were at Tulagi resting from a run
up the "Slot," the call to General Quarters sounded. We
weighed anchor and got the hell out of the harbor. We then
went to Modified General Quarters (one-half the crew at battle
stations). I was on the raised deck of number 4 gun working
out with Alan Levinson when our signal lights started blinking
at the shore of Guadalcanal near Lunga Point. Our guns came
around fast. We could see a small craft near the shore, but it
was not answering back. At the time, Captain Brown was trying
to deep-six some Japanese supplies drifting in on the tide and
said, "Sink him." Buzz, bang—two shots straddled the little
guy. That son of a gun moved then! The rooster tail from the
screws must have gone 20 feet into the air with his blinker
lights flashing back to say he was a friendly PT boat.

Captain Brown hardly ever left the bridge at sea. He was
always calm and quiet even when we were under attack. He
chewed gum and wore a baseball-type cap with a green visor.
The harder the action, the faster he chewed. He looked like a
professional gambler. The enlisted men on the bridge called
him, "Rack 'em up, stack 'em up, shoot 'em down Brown,"
but not to his face. No one joked in his presence.

One day, Admiral Halsey's sign was gone. We found out
later that the Admiral ordered it taken down because women
should not be exposed to that kind of language. It had to go
because our First Lady, Eleanor Roosevelt, had left home and
safety to make a trip to the battlefields of the Pacific to see
first-hand how things were going. What a great and gracious

lady! The war had displaced her family as much as anyone's, and here she came into harm's way to see us.

Willis Martin Norman was a bowler. He only bowled in the machine shop while Machinist's Mate First Class R. H. Swan was at work. Swan didn't like anyone. It seemed he even hated himself. Norman bowled very quietly to keep from disturbing Swan. He kept his scorecard on an imaginary board with a nonexisting pen and used bowling balls that you couldn't see on an alley that wasn't there. A strike made no more noise than a single pin. At times when Norman was bowling, people would gather around and talk about his game and try to find out what his score was. He never did tell us. Neither would he tell us when he made a strike; we just had to guess at it. He was also a fine amateur photographer and took some of the best pictures of the ship.

Chief Water Tender Jim Knight had a salty look even in the shower. Covered with selected tattoos, he had a look that said, "I was here in the beginning and the Navy was made for me! Who the hell are you and what do you want?" When he was on deck, we all gathered around to hear his bullshit and, sometimes, true Navy tales. Every man aboard loved him; he only tolerated us.

One day, eleven LSTs came into sight over the horizon. Chief Knight was up on deck with everybody gathered around him as usual. Someone called his attention to the LSTs. He looked at them with kind of a gleam in his eye and a grin on his face and said, "Yup, Halsey will attack Rabaul now. We've got eleven barges, and that old bastard will use them!" No one disputed what he said. We all had a great love for Halsey. But in this case, Halsey never used them for Rabaul because we lost most of them up the "Slot."

During nightly raids up the "Slot," we had an average speed of 20 to 30 knots. Many times we had to get in and out in a hurry to dodge daytime raids by enemy planes and get back to our air cover. The battlefield was 600 miles long from Guadalcanal to the northern Solomons, or at times to Rabaul. The best thing I remember about night watch was the night rations. The bread was usually still hot and served with canned salmon or Spam, which everyone hated. The bread was the best in the world; we all loved the bakers who worked at night.

When a full General Quarters was in effect, everyone was at their battle stations with all watertight doors closed and battened down as tightly as possible. The Captain was on the bridge, with control of every action taken by anyone aboard. All units were connected to the battle talker who relayed the Captain's orders to all stations. The engine rooms and fire-rooms were given their orders by a special signal on an indicator, which showed the various speeds to be used, such as one-third, flank, or full. It also could signal to back down and stop. These signals were all used to throw off the accuracy of the enemy. For example, if a plane was diving at us, we might go to flank speed, hard right or left turn. If we had damage, we would go to a full stop since water flows in faster through a hole when a ship is moving. Pilots get distracted when you are moving and the guns are all throwing up a blizzard of steel. With a good crew operating in this way, it is very hard for a lone plane to get you. We once went from flank speed to a hard right to stop to flank speed again and hard left while laying the cold hand on three Japanese planes diving at us, all in a matter of nine minutes.

Looking back over 20 months of action in the Solomons, I could see that we had all changed. I was both physically and mentally tough, working out every day. I ran around the deck like it was a track, punched my timing bag incessantly, and carried a tilted chip on my shoulder.

I was assigned a battle station briefly in the steering engine room and the throttle board, but 99 percent of my time was on the lower-level forward engine room. The temperatures endured in the firerooms and engine rooms were a constant 100°F or more. Everyone below decks had heat rash and jungle rot, especially those who worked in the engine room and fire-room. To give you an example of how safe it was, I had one of the stations nearest the bottom of the ship. The deaerated feed tank (DFT) was located above me with 800 gallons to 1000 gallons of feed, that is, water made from condensed steam, ready to be pumped back to the boilers, reheated, and used again. Steam lines were all about and, if they were ruptured, you could cook in about a second. The main condenser, main turbine, and auxiliary turbines were maintained at a vacuum of close to 29 inches. A hit on the main condenser would cause an implosion due to the vacuum. At the same time, steam at 600°F to 800°F could cook you, explosions could blast you, and water could drown you. Thus, if you received a hit of any kind, the engine room was more dangerous than the shell, torpedo, or bomb that did the original damage. And you still had to contend with the seawater coming in on you.

The after steering room contained the pumps and motors that hydraulically moved the rudders to steer the ship. This room was located aft of the number 5 gun mount and below the after 20-mm and 40-mm machine guns. It was directly above both the ship's propellers and the two rudders on the outside of the hull just aft of the propellers. A machinist's mate and electrician's mate were stationed in the after steering room during battle conditions to take over steering the ship in case the bridge was hit and steering control was lost by the helmsman on the bridge. These stations were as close to hell as a man could get in this world. The men would rush to the after steering room when the General Quarters alarm sounded, dog the watertight door down, and close the topside escape hatch. One of the men would don the earphones. Then, all hell would explode. The number 5 gun mount would start to shake things up. The 20-mm and 40-mm guns would start to fire, dumping several hundred shell cases per minute on the quarter-inch deck plate. When the ship's propellers would speed up, the vibration would shake everything. The propeller shafts would start making a warping sound as if they wanted to leave the shaft mounts. The rudders and hydraulic lines would moan in their labors, and underwater explosions would hit the hull just outside. If you were there, your skivvies would be just a little damp where you almost wet yourself. Later, when battle stations were secured, stinking salty sweat would cover your whole body like a warm, wet rag. You would have just played a passive part in a fight at sea. Electrician's Mate First Class Keith Rossiter was my partner in this battle station.

Ammunition handling rooms, located deep inside the ship, were crowded, hot, and noisy. We had five. When we were firing all out (22 rounds per minute), extended action would work you so hard that, when you had a chance to rest, you would just sink to the deck where you were. In one three-week period, we laid out 4100 rounds of 5-inch 38 shells and thousands of rounds of 20-mm and 40-mm fire. One seaman, Carl Watts of North Carolina, refused to go back to the handling room after he was wounded during an air attack when stacked ammunition fell on his legs, injuring him. The way Carl tells it, the ammunition was stacked against the bulkhead and held up by brackets bolted to the bulkhead. The rack he was using was partially undone and the ship was at flank speed and turning. When the plane hit nearby during this high-speed turn, 5-inch 38 shells flew out of the rack and hit him, knocking him down and partially covering his legs and body. Carl knew the shells could blow up, and he said the handling room closed in on him until it was no larger than a shoebox. He told the doctor and gunnery officer he couldn't go back there any more; they gave him a battle station topside.

The gunners also suffered from the same lack of protection. Their gun turrets were only splinter shields made of three-eighths inch steel plate like the rest of the ship. The 20-mm and 40-mm gunners had even less protection than the 5-inch 38s. No matter what happened, they had to stay the course of the fight. If they ran, they ensured their own destruction. Besides, if they did run and survive, they still had to face their shipmates who might kill them. The ammunition-handlers were stuck in the real hot spot of the ship; no one had to tell them it could blow. So you see, each man felt safe in his own little gateway to hell and sorrow for his shipmates in other dangerous spots.

June 19, 1943, we attacked our first submarine. We escorted a group of cruisers on a night bombardment up the

"Slot." On our return trip, cruiser *Columbus* picked up a surface target about 15 miles to our port side. *Saufley* received orders to attack. The engines revved up to flank speed, and we headed straight for him. At about 1½ miles, we opened fire with our 5-inch 38s and missed him. Our radar operators were new at using the radar, and our failure to use flares during night attacks caused us to miss until the radar men became better trained for night fights. When the submarine dived, we made three depth charge attacks and then lost him on the sonar. After the war was over, the Japanese said they had lost a submarine in the area of our attack but the Navy awarded the kill to another ship.

Our only form of air-conditioning was fresh air from one 3-inch line in the engineer's quarters, port and starboard. It didn't work well because everyone had cut holes in it by their bunks and put pasteboard deflectors in each hole. The ones nearest the intake had air while the others had none. It didn't matter much because the air itself was 100°F or more at all times. A steam bath would have seemed just as cooling.

Most of us slept topside to beat the heat. We slept on the decks and life rafts, under the gun mounts, or anywhere we could. One man slept in a hammock slung under the search light platform. I don't remember his name, but I still worry about his falling. The general consensus around the ship was that he had to be crazy. I laid on a Navy blanket on the deck with my shoes as a pillow. I always wore my uniform shirt and dungarees so I'd be ready to go to General Quarters at all times. It was most shocking to be sleeping on the deck and have the firing start before the battle alarm sounded. Tracers from the 20-mm and 40-mm guns lit up the sky. The sharp, loud sound from the 5-inch 38s overpowered everything except the battle alarm. Waves of concussion from the fast-firing guns pulled at your clothes as if they were trying to undress you. Your balance was off because of the roll of the ship and blast of the shells. You had to put your shoes on before entering the engine room because the steel ladders and hot floor plates would either cut or burn your feet. The old-timers were used to this routine, but the new boots were confused the first time the battle alarm sounded. They would be run down by sailors going hell-for-leather for their battle stations.

Once while we were on a night run up the "Slot," Jim Fagan and I were sitting on the fantail life raft. It was cloudy with a low ceiling. When a Japanese bomber came over the clear patch of sky, we could have hit him with a baseball he was so close. I thought we were the only ones to see him. We ran to report it and were told that radar had him in sight. "Couldn't we see the gun mounts follow him in and out?" We had orders not to shoot at lone planes that night. It made us wonder how often this kind of thing happened. We would find out soon enough.

During July 1943, Destroyer Squadron 22 was looking for trouble up the "Slot." We were steaming fast on the lookout for the "Tokyo Express." Our General Quarters crew for the director consisted of Lieutenant Marshal, Seaman First Class Art Cyr, Seaman First Class Saddler, and Fire Controlman Second Class John J. Larned. Our observer was Chief Torpedoman Howard Owen. One of the lookouts spotted a plane coming in low and fast on our starboard side. The 20-mm guns were the only ones to fire, but they were not effective. Larned could hear everything on the phone circuit to the bridge, guns, and control room. Joe Dowling, a young helmsman, saw the torpedo drop and grabbed Captain Brown's shoulder saying, "Captain Brown, he's dropped a damn torpedo on our deck." Captain Brown's voice came in clear and cold: "So I see, son." The torpedo was going to hit us between the forward engine room or just below the bridge. Calm as could be, Captain Brown came on the open phone circuit with an order to the helmsman to change course. Larned said the torpedo ran deep under the ship. The angel in our rigging had saved us all for another day, with the help of calm Captain Brown!

Red Cotter was captain of number 1 gun mount. Once, when the hot-shell man was missing and there was a misfire set to explode, Jim Fagan came running by, took the hot shell, threw it overboard, and kept running to his battle station! He would help a man in trouble anywhere at any time.

One afternoon at Modified General Quarters, we had a submarine contact and dropped depth charges several times. After that, things were quiet for a while. I was having a bad time with jungle rot all over my crotch and backside and was laying with my chest and shoulders in the shade of the number 4 5-inch gun mount with my pants and shorts down to my knees sunning this rash. Suddenly everyone started to point and yell. The guns swung around and started to fire as fast as they could. I got full concussion from at least four rounds. Before I could move out, the submarine had surfaced and looked as big as *Saufley*. We were hitting the submarine with a steady stream of 20-mm, 40-mm, and 5-inch 38 shells, all placed right in his conning tower. At the same time, a damn PBY (number 41 from VP 23) came in so close that it's a wonder our shells didn't get him too. The PBY dropped a bomb right where we were shooting. Everyone started to cuss; it looked like that son of a bitch was trying to steal our submarine. The Japanese submarine RO-103 was destroyed with no survivors; Lieutenant Commander Fujisawa and all his crew were gone before I could get my pants up and buckle my belt. Captain Brown felt we should have received full credit for the kill, but the PBY was given half credit.

We carried out a series of bombardments all the way up the "Slot." We went into Empress Augusta Bay in conjunction with the PT boats, which made spot attacks close to shore, while we shot heavier shells over their heads. Our crew had become so adept at handling this 2050 tons of three-eighths inch plate that it was like riding in a speedboat. Also, luck hung around our necks like a fine necklace.

Our war in the Solomons was small compared to the war in Europe, but our fights were for all the marbles. It was as if we were lost with only the string of islands to cling to. All of us went through moods and mind changes. You would be playing checkers with a friend one day, and the next day you couldn't stand him. To avoid a fuss, you just stayed clear of him that day. The engineers would gather in the machine shop at night and shoot the breeze, including Shaw, Newby, Berry, Stoneham, Pappy Deer, Fagan, Swan, DeGuiseppe, Dalland, Norman, O'Reilly, and more. The names changed but the stories were the same each night: home, girls, shore leave, food, ice cream, different ships we served on, things that had happened, things yet to happen, but most of all, home. One thing we talked about was how to pick up girls. Combat ribbons were the thing most of us thought would attract the girls. I never got to wear mine. When we finally went to San Francisco for six weeks, I bought mine and lost them all on the first liberty. The girls seemed to know who had seen combat without any ribbons. I found out later the combat veterans hardly ever wore their ribbons, and the dance-hall heroes all had quite a few to wear.

Machinist's Mate First Class R. H. Swan thought he owned the machine shop. Swan was bitter about a court-martial he received for getting a severe sunburn before the war. He said the court-martial kept him from making chief. He could have been right. Senior Electrician's Mate First Class Shaw kept Swan from running us out of our nighttime gathering place. Shaw and Stoneham both made chief. Since there was no room in the chief's quarters, they bunked with us until they were transferred to a new ship. One night, the two men decided to talk Swan out of the shop, so all they talked about was what would happen to Swan if we were hit by a torpedo: how it would ruin the lathe and mess up all of his drawing, stop him from his work, mix his body into the machinery, and maybe force his brains out through the watertight door or shove his ass so high on his shoulders he would have to stand on his head to crap. They also suggested the torpedo would shove his head down through his ass and the Navy could slice him up for grommets. It had Swan so upset he just left the shop and didn't come in at night anymore. That's how it happened that we took control of the machine shop at night!

⚓ 7 ⚓

IN THE LAND DOWN UNDER

JULY 1943 – AUGUST 1943

July and August found Saufley *engaged in assault operations against New Georgia and escort missions to the New Hebrides and Vella Lavella. On 31 August, she received minor damage, but no casualties, from near misses by shore batteries in the "Slot", the narrow body of water that separates the central Solomons.*
—*from* The Dictionary of American Naval Fighting Ships

T he most hateful watch of all was the 4 AM to 8 AM morning watch. I would leave the engine room with sweat over my body like sugar on a glazed donut, hurry back to the washroom, bathe, wash my clothes, put clean dungarees on, and hang the ones I washed to dry. Other people would be in the chow line only half-awake and tired from the nighttime calls to General Quarters and the heat that drained you of all energy. The morning sun would be looking like a bloody bubble in a peapot. The chow line formed and went down to the chow hall where the food was kept hot on steam tables. The humidity was almost unbearable. A typical breakfast would be scrambled, powdered eggs (always watery), soggy toast, Spam (fried on one side and raw on the other), and coffee that made you hotter or powdered lemonade that made you sick. The thing that hurt most of all was the sight of mess boys going by with sunny-side-up eggs, cinnamon rolls, bacon, and orange juice for the officers' mess.

The officers and chiefs had their own special messes. Although the chiefs' mess had its own cook, they cooked and ate out of our sight. But the officers had mess boys, who cooked food like ham, bacon, eggs, and nice steaks in our galley. The officers also enjoyed ice cream, strawberries, fresh vegetables, lettuce, and tomatoes. Even though the mess boys could have gone to the officers' mess up the starboard side, they went up the port side along the full length of our chow line. It was a constant, nagging reminder that we were first-class citizens caught in a third-class situation; the officers' mess boys quietly rubbed it in with every meal. This situation caused resentment among the enlisted men and the theft of lots of the officers' food.

You can't begin to understand what it was like to do without fresh food, ice cream, steak, fresh eggs, and bacon. Even cigarettes could not be obtained at times. What we considered fresh food was Spam and dehydrated potatoes and eggs. All of our mutton and beef came from Australia. I know for a fact that in Sydney they had good steaks and mutton, but none of it was ever shipped to us. Many times I saw the cooks deep-six halves of beef and mutton that were too tough to eat. When we got an availability alongside a destroyer tender, we could get candy, real cold drinks that fizzed, writing materials, and spare parts of all kinds. If you had a friend aboard the tender, you could eat in the crew's mess. I had one friend on *Whitney* who worked in the ice machines and gave me all the ice cream I could eat.

Taking on stores was a nice thing to do. When we took on stores, the supply officers never had to ask for our help. Everyone aboard was willing to help for each division needed canned fruit, ham, salmon, stew, or anything that could be stored and hidden for future use. The forward engine room and fireroom had the best scavengers on the ship. Our hatches were in the best location for scavenging, and the bilges and other nooks and crannies were the best places to hide our stashes. At first, the storekeepers and supply officers tried to stop us, but in the final analysis they had to give up and order enough food for us to get our little bit of pilferage along with the regular supplies. It must have created one hell of a problem for the supply officers. I can still see Jim Fagan and Dennis O'Reilly making quick right turns into the entrance and handing off packages of food to cohorts who passed it right down into the bilges. Fagan could really cook a fine stew that smelled all over the ship. Besides, it was good psychology for us to win at this little game.

Right after breakfast, the line at sick bay would form. The pharmacist's mate would sit in a chair and hold sick call. About 90 percent of sick call problems involved skin trouble. The treatment was to drop your pants, get swabbed around your crotch with something that burned like hell (but helped), turn around with your pants still down, bend over, and get swabbed on your backside. The pharmacist's mate would usually make a mistake and get some on your sensitive gear hanging down. This mistake made you want to stay away from sick bay.

One morning I was in line for sick call just behind J. R. Berry. He jumped all over Harold Wright, the duty pharmacist's mate, talking real nasty to him about a wart on the crown of his head. Berry was tough; he had been a great high-school wrestler. It was the first time I had ever seen him mad. Wright was tall and thin, regular Navy, and had completed a hitch or two in service before the war. He had volunteered to serve with the Marines ashore and had been wounded two or three times. He worked out with me with the gloves. He was also tough, weighing about 150 pounds, and not afraid of anyone. I figured a fight was coming, and a good one! Wright was calm as could be. When Berry reached him, he looked all around for a good five minutes and came up with a small brown bottle. Opening the bottle, he used an eye dropper to put a drop on Berry's wart. Once open, the bottle started to smoke, so Wright shut it quickly. The wart turned white and started to smoke like a phosphorus shell. Berry got a shocked look on his face, wheeled and ran like a deer to the shower room, pushed someone to the side, and jumped in the shower, clothes and all. The wart went away and never came back. Old Wright smiled and kept on treating us. His treatment was very effective.

Mailman Ed Duffy was our ship's postmaster. Mail call was a happy time for every person aboard ship. (I did not write to anyone except Mom and that was one-sided.) So many great things happened at mail call that Duffy was like a king. When we had been at sea for a while and came back to port, Ed's job was to get the mail. Sometimes before we stopped, he would be in the motor whaleboat and lowered into the water. When he returned, the mail was always sorted and delivered to each division. Everyone would gather around, and each man's name was called as his mail was pulled from the bag. One had to remain until the mailbag was empty. If you couldn't get to the bag, you just yelled when your name was called. Then your mail would be passed back from one to another up in the air over everyone's head until you received it.

I would sit and watch the people who were married and engaged, how their faces would light up when they got their mail. Einhorn, Elliott, and Englehardt always got letters from their girls, which they would open up right where they stood, their faces as happy as a five-year-old at Christmas. I watched my Italian friends closely because, whenever they received a care package from home, they always shared it with me. A care package from an Italian Mom was just like a visit from an angel. I especially watched Paul DeRosa whose wife was named Rosa. He received the best packages of all.

I could also tell when one received bad news in the mail. I didn't know which hurt the most: death news or "Dear Johns." At times, I hurt for them when they cried. At the same time, I would be glad that all my friends were aboard ship; no love letter or no "Dear Johns" for me. We were just shipmates with a war to fight. Ed Duffy is dead now, but he did a good job that I'm sure he enjoyed.

One day after we had received mail and I was busy on the fantail watching happy faces and looking for care packages,

Captain Brown had me lay up to his cabin. He and Mr. Cochran were there together staring at me. The Captain gave me a letter from Mom together with his instructions to write to her! In fact, I would give a letter to Mr. Cochran once a week as long as I was in his ship and under his command, or he would make my life miserable. I didn't even realize I hadn't written home for such a long time. I was ashamed of myself and told them both so.

The evaporators were above my duty station in the engine room. Their main function was to make fresh water from seawater. The man on watch had a gauge that showed the varying degrees of salinity. If the indicator was in the green, everything was OK. But if it started going to the red area, there was hell to pay as saltwater was going into what fresh water we already had in the tanks.

Old Chief Brinkman had been recalled from retirement. He was so mean and cantankerous that Mr. Cochran put him in charge of the evaporators and lubricating oil for the main engines. He was real good at it and kept a supply of good water for us. He renovated our oil supply and kept the main engines going for the duration of the war. He was one of the best men we had.

I found a valve on the lower level that turned the gauge off on the salinity of water going to our fresh water tanks. It would go into the red, even though the water was good. I guess at least three or four times during a watch, I would cause the gauge to go red. The man on watch would be frantic and finally call Chief B. J. Brinkman from his sleep. When Old Chief Brinkman's feet hit the floor plates and the gauge was in the green, he would cuss and pitch a fit that was most magnificent to see. Machinist's Mate Third Class N. H. Huffine from Johnson City, Tennessee, was the man I usually pulled this on. I loved him like a brother, but with a friend like me, he didn't need any enemies.

We had one man at all times called the "Captain of the Head." It was his duty to clean the head, every square inch of it from the crapper seats to the mirrors. He was unhappy at all times because we picked on him and got mad when he closed off parts of the head. It was a dirty job, and somebody had to do it. The enlisted men's head had a line of washbasins down the center on a steel frame, with basins on each side to allow several men to brush their teeth and so on. Urinals and toilets were built along the outside port bulkhead. The toilets were long and trough-shaped with black U-shaped seats and a continuous supply of saltwater flowing in at the forward end and out into the sea again. You sat right by each other with no privacy whatsoever. Many rolls of toilet paper, hung on a steel pipe, were behind the toilets. It was very efficient since a man moved on as soon as he possibly could. No one ever took a rest on the toilets because you could get burned! Someone would get to the forward part of the trough, light a loosely crushed handful of toilet paper, and drop it into the flow of saltwater. As it drifted down the line singeing body hair, shipmates would come up cussing; they were most proficient at this. I always waited until I could sit at the forward end.

The showers were oriented to the masses. Fresh water was turned on at change of watch times only if we had a plentiful supply. Otherwise, we had saltwater showers. At times, five or six men would be using the urinals. I always thought of the time an electrician hooked a small hand generator to our dockside urinals in the Brooklyn Navy yard. I was caught in this trap along with several others. It was very funny to the people watching, but not to the ones getting shocked. We would have hurt the prankster if we had caught him. I never used that particular urinal again.

We visited Sydney twice during the Solomons' knockdown. Usually, we would hire a taxi as a group to save money and then have to get out and push it to get over a hill. Taxis in Sydney operated on coke burning in the trunk. I never knew how they modified the motors. The taxis ran off the gas produced by the coke burning in the trunk of the car and worked well on level pavement. They could climb a hill with two passengers, but if there were more than two people, you had to get out and push! Cops or civilians would help us get over the hills. The cops were some of the best people in Sydney.

One of our Irish sailors got drunk with an Irish milkman in Sydney who used a horse-drawn wagon to make his deliveries. After the milkman passed out on the wagon seat, our drunken sailor got off when the horse stopped for the pier where the ship was tied up. The horse waited long enough to let the sailor off and then kept on to each delivery point where he would pause again before moving on to the next point. Although the milkman made his rounds, no milk was delivered.

One morning, I came back from liberty and found my old buddy Fagan in someone else's bunk at the bottom of the ladder. He was wearing a pair of girl's panties and an Australian 9th Division wool overcoat. When he went to sleep on shore, the girl he was with had taken off with all his clothes, leaving only her panties. She even took his shoes. He found the coat in her closet. He never said how he got back to the ship.

O. R. Elliott, Rod Berry, and I stayed with three girls in their apartment in Sydney. There were three more apartments on the floor with boys from *Saufley* and girls from Sydney and the outback. To take a bath, you had to draw the water in the bathtub, which sat high off the floor, and heat the water with a gas burner underneath the tub. One of the girls from the outback had a bad odor. Her boyfriend told her so and gave her a bottle of Lysol. She heated the water and poured the whole bottle into the tub. Fortunately, she didn't get in. We all had a good laugh. About 15 days later, he went to Dr. Jones who finally had to operate on him. I don't know what the girl had, but he had the male equivalent of a D&C.

One of our officers met an Aussie girl who was a high-ranking lady athlete and a beauty. He bragged about this girl right up to the day he had to call Dr. Jones to his cabin. Sydney was good to us, but the Navy should have handed out Purple Hearts.

One of my best friends was 17 years old when he joined

the Navy at the start of the war. He came from a very large and poor family. He was also a virgin and admitted this fact to everyone. A whole group of young sailors went to him and admitted that they, too, had never had a woman. They went ashore as a group in Sydney. I don't know what happened, but several of them visited the shanker mechanic after we sailed.

E. T. Thompson was a son of the old South and one of the sharpest-looking sailors I've ever seen. His hair, clothes, and shoes were neat at all times. He was from the remnants of the Asiatic Four-Piper Destroyer Fleet. Everything about him shined! He was a machinist's mate second class and was the best man I've ever seen on a throttle board. He could answer a signal in seconds and always had the engines turning at the right RPM. He was also the luckiest gambler on the ship and always had thousands of dollars in his money belt. He had a ring made from corrosion-resistant steel mounted with Australian diamonds. The ring was just as polished as his shoes. The dice always worked in his favor. Some crew members accused him of using crooked dice, but no one ever caught him. When he went ashore, he always had someone he trusted keep his money belt because within an hour, he was the drunkest and crummiest sailor in the world: foul-mouthed and mean with a thousand-yard stare that made you feel uncomfortable. Thompson had been in all the early battles against the Japanese. He had also sent thousands of dollars home. Later, he was transferred back to new construction and was killed by a taxicab in New York City.

Navy dungarees were the most loved possession anyone had. When we bought new ones, we wrote our names on the shirt and pants with bleach. Then, the process of washing started. I tied mine to a rope and hung them from the fantail of the ship to let the saltwater bleach them. After at least ten hours of towing behind the ship, they would change to the worn look that everyone wants today. Then I gave them a good washing in a bucket of bleached water. After that, I loved them like a wife. Truly, if we had been given a choice, many of us would have worn them ashore instead of dress blues or whites.

"Jernigan's washing machine", actually the view from the fantail with the Saufley at 22 knots.

One night, when I came off the watch and went to the head to shower and wash my clothes, I was almost knocked out by the smell. One of the water tenders, whose job it was to check the salinity in the boiler water, drank the alcohol mixed with the soap used for checking the water salinity. He thought all the soap was out of the alcohol, believing the scuttlebutt that straining the alcohol through bread would take all the soap out. It was one of the times scuttlebutt was wrong. The drunker he became, the sicker he became. It was one big drunk and one continuous enema. His own top bunk was filthy with feces as were the two bunks below, the footlockers, and adjacent bunks. He was sitting on a toilet seat nasty from head to toe, and even had it in his hair. Everyone in the engineering compartment was mad as hell. I'm sure he would have been thrown overboard except for the one thought in everyone's head: Who would clean it up? He did clean it up and was then transferred when we reached Tulagi.

Chief Machinist's Mate D. R. Huie was a fisherman. He was assigned to the after engine room. His second duty station was on the fantail fishing. He would use a long line that reached to the bottom with two, three, or four hooks to catch several small bottom-feeding fish at once. He never caught any large ones until this one night. After many tries, he hooked up a great length of line to a 5-inch shell casing for a cork with a sharpened and barbed meat hook from the butcher shop and a piece of raw meat weighing 20 pounds or more. Then he threw it over the side of the fantail and let the sea have it for the night. I don't remember where we were anchored. The next morning when I came off the morning watch and started back to our crew's quarters, I saw that Chief Huie had caught and hung a great shark on one of the davits used for handling the rolloff ashcans for anti-submarine work. This big shark was hanging by his tail with his guts run out on the deck while crew members stood around in wonder at the size of this great denizen of the blue waters. Before this episode, one form of recreation when we were in harbor had been swimming. The motor whaleboat would circle the ship with a sharpshooter aboard with a loaded rifle at the ready just in case. Both the crew and officers used to swim, but I don't believe we ever had another swimming party after that. These swimming parties had been good recreation with many men diving from the wing of the bridge. One of them, Frank S. Edwards, in different times would have earned many honors as a high diver.

At Ulithi, Chief Huie fished above the area where one of our ammunition ships had exploded. He caught a human leg. I never saw him fishing again.

Saufley went in commission early and was lucky enough to get experienced petty officers from all over the Navy. Most of them stayed with her for the war's duration. The Navy continuously transferred men back to the States to help commission new ships and train new crews, but we were lucky and kept many of the best men. Each group of men who went back to the States had to start anew with new men. Their competency at this training task was a factor in the success of future battles.

One of our shipmates fell overboard, just at dusk. He was leaning against the lifeline cables strung around the ship when one of them parted. He fell right into the sea. Fortunately, the ship wasn't going too fast or he would have been sucked into one of the screws. Captain Cochran did something then that I admired him for. He put the ship and the lives of every man on board at risk when he stopped in a war zone, searched for the man, even turning the searchlights on when it got darker, until we found him. Many commanders wouldn't do this knowing that Captain McVey, the commanding officer of cruiser *Indianapolis*, was court-martialed when his cruiser was sunk by a submarine between Saipan and the Philippines. They said he was at fault for not running a zig-zag course. Captain Cochran would have really been in trouble had we been sunk while dead in the water looking for one lonely little seaman who had gone overboard. It was a great act of courage on his part.

⚓ **8** ⚓

HELL UNLEASHED

AUGUST 1943 – DECEMBER 1943

At 1011 on 15 September, while Saufley *was en route to Espiritu Santo in company with* Montgomery *(DD-121) and two merchantmen, a torpedo wake was sighted. As* Montgomery's *sound gear was inoperative,* Saufley *initiated a search down the track of the torpedo wake. Over the period of the next three and one-half hours, she delivered five separate depth charge attacks against the submarine. At 1443, the Japanese submarine,* RO-101, *surfaced.*

Saufley's *five-inch batteries and machine guns opened up on the conning tower of the submarine. A Catalina flying boat moved in and dropped two depth charges. The first charge missed the target by about 40 feet, but the second one hit it. When the splash subsided, the submarine was gone. An underwater explosion was heard; and, by 1735, diesel oil, covering an area of approximately one square mile, marked the grave of* RO-101.

During the remainder of September and well into October, Saufley *was engaged in night antibarge patrols between Kolombangara and Choiseul. She sank four barges during this period but sustained damage from Japanese aerial bombs on the night of 1 October which resulted in the death of two crew members and the wounding of 11 others.—from* The Dictionary of American Naval Fighting Ships

L**ate** in 1943, we were getting new men, ships, and material in greater amounts, and we were on the offensive. The enemy never knew where we would hit them next.

At Vella Lavella, Solomon Islands, we had some very rough

fights. By late 1943, the Japanese were through with any thoughts of victory and just wanted to get their men off the islands. The American troops began landing at Vella Lavella on August 15, 1943. *Saufley* was the screening ship for the LCIs and assisted in repelling enemy air attacks that night. We were rocked by six underwater explosions that dimmed the lights. With radical maneuvering of the ship and the blasting of guns, you had to grab something and hold on. The bilge water rushed from side to side. Loose articles moved about on the deck plates only to come back from the opposite side when high-speed maneuvering caused the ship to lean in a different direction.

Everyone sweated during combat. Sweat during battle had an odor much stronger than regular sweat. You could see it on foreheads and lips. It also seemed that the ship's sides sweated more when maneuvering at high speed with all the guns firing. If you were below decks, you could tell when the fight moved in closer by the type of gunfire. First the 5-inch, then the 40-mm, and then the 20-mm would cut loose. When the 20-mm fired all 60 shots and stopped for a second to reload, you could tell the fight was close and getting closer. There was nothing to do except suck up your gut and, in my case, I would recite my own little motto from boyhood: "I don't give a damn if I do die, do die; just so I see a little juice fly, juice fly." I hadn't died yet at this point, and I had seen a lot of juice fly all over the Solomons. I always got a high during a fight.

One day, we had escorted three LSTs loaded to the water-line with supplies for the Seabees at Vella Lavella where they were building an airbase. The LSTs were beached and in the process of unloading when Chief Hastings called me to the top of the ladder. He warned me that we had picked up 40 to 60 planes on our radar at a distance of 80 miles and then lost them. He told me to check everything on the lower level. We only had two other destroyers with us, and I was worried an air attack would sink us all. The boys in the forward fireroom put the superheaters on line, going to 800°F steam. At flank speed, our turbines came up to a high-pitched whine. We began maneuvering, but the guns were silent. I became very curious about what was going on and climbed a vertical ladder on the starboard side to the upper deck. From there, I climbed another vertical ladder to a small hatch used as an emergency exit. Spinning the wheel in the center, I threw the hatch up and stuck my head and shoulders out. Just at that moment, every gun on the ship opened up to the starboard side at four dive bombers releasing bombs. Cork and cordite were flying everywhere. The blast of the guns nearly took my eyeballs, eyelids, and ears off. I went back to the lower level faster than a prairie dog can get in a hole. For the next 10 minutes, every gun kept up a steady fire. The planes attacked in groups of four but did not score a single hit because of our intense fire and luck. In a 10-day period, we were attacked nine times but sustained no damage. We shot down four planes in the first attack alone. Captain Brown received a Silver Star for this operation, which happened between August 1 and 16, 1943.

Being in the engine room during battle reminded me of doing ironwork at a great height. When you reach the top and the clouds floating by make you dizzy, you can climb down not feeling the least bit ashamed. Being in the engine room when hell's popping topside made you want to haul ass up the ladder. Only a stubborn pride kept you anchored to the deck plates until the fear passed.

On August 16, 1943, we were ordered to assist in another action off Vella Lavella but were recalled when the beachhead was brought under heavy air attack. During this action, we laid to in the water to pick up survivors from LST 396, which was on fire and sinking. All our rescue nets were over the side for men in the water to climb aboard our ship. Our motor whale-boat was in the water and was picking up people left and right in the face of flying debris, fire, and heavy air attack. Chief Colleran let us go topside one at a time to see the fight. When it was my time to go up, I ran up from the forward engine room hatch so I could see Tony Eabon's gun, which was going full blast at something I could not see. It was a strangely beautiful sight, all the tracers in the air and the burning LST. Looking out, I could see men helping survivors up the rescue nets onto the deck and then right back to our aid station in the enlisted men's washroom. *Saufley* picked up 93 men that day. The only one to die was a pharmacist's mate. It could have been much worse.

Let me describe this man's burial at sea since it was typical for the Navy in wartime. Burial at sea is sad because it is so casual, brutal, beautiful, and final. No one wanted to be the main actor. When the doctors pronounced a man dead and we were near a base, the dead man was put in the refrigerator room. At sea, loving hands prepared him for burial. Canvas from the boatswain's locker was cut and sewn shut at the bottom. Two 5-inch shells were put inside the canvas to make it sink. A small hole at the top allowed the air to escape and the body to sink. The boatswain, or someone he appointed, sewed the body into the canvas. The canvas bag was placed on the side of the ship at the fantail. A prayer was said, taps were blown, and a gun salute fired. The board on which the man rested was tilted until the body went feet first into the sea, leaving only the covering flag. Many tears fell as the deceased started the long fall to the bottomless deep on a ride that lasts forever, a most final and solemn act.

Submarine chaser 1266 picked up the rest of the survivors of the August 16, 1943, attack. The 1266 was laying to just as we were on our port side. I don't know if she was wood or steel, but she was very small and looked like a fishing boat. Someone on her bridge had a tommy gun cradled in his arm. Above his head was a name, "Little Joe," painted in black against a white background with a pair of dice showing the number 4 the hard way. On the next morning, we were attacked by eight to ten dive bombers coming at us out of the sun. They dropped two bombs close aboard. We shot one plane down, which crashed close by the beachhead. We were almost out of ammunition at this point and everyone was dead tired when we finally hauled out for Tulagi to let the passengers off, take on more ammunition and fuel, and return at 30 knots. We had been in almost constant action for 72 hours with little chance to sleep. It's a wonder we made it back with everyone so sleepy.

On the way back to Tulagi, we passed a PT boat that had been holed at a slight angle from port to starboard on the forward bow. I don't know if it was a torpedo launched too close, a bomb, or a shell, but it had not exploded, The crew of the PT boat was extremely happy to weave around and show us their war wound. The whole crew was topside and as happy as if they had good sense.

Our anchorage at Tulagi harbor was not too far from the creek where the PT boats tied up at night. We could always hear the low, deep-breathing growl of their ~~Chrysler~~ *Packard* motors when one of them started. The crew on *Saufley* would watch as the little plywood monsters throttled out at low speed. The crews waved to us, and the boat kicked up a rooster tail when they opened up and headed up the "Slot." The men wore cut-off dungarees and were mostly young with partial beards and deep tans. Our future President, John F. Kennedy, was in this group in PT 109. He visited us occasionally along with most of the other PT boat officers. They would tie up at our fantail and come aboard, always going to the wardroom to get some chow.

On August 17, 1943, we had one of our best shooting days ever. We hit several planes that probably didn't make it back to their base; they were smoking and losing altitude as they left. At the start of the attack, we saw eight to ten dive bombers coming at us out of the sun. The machine guns fired at the two planes that dropped bombs close aboard and pulled out and away, while the 5-inch 38s were firing at the two planes attacking the beach. The gunnery officer then changed fire to a single plane going out from our starboard side. After being hit by a 5-inch shell burst, it crashed close to the beach. Our gunnery officer, Lieutenant W. J. Martin from Illinois, had taken over from our first gunnery officer, Lieutenant Bangert, who was largely responsible for our good training at gunnery.

You could tell a good gunner's tracers from a bad one. He

would lead the plane well and his tracers would look like they would miss the plane by a mile. The tracers would start to form a line that arched out in front of the plane and started back bent in the shape of a strung longbow. I don't know if what I saw was an illusion brought on by motion, but the good gunner's tracers looked like a miss halfway to the target. Then they seemed to bend back to the plane and hit it. We were lucky with men like Doughty, Duprey, Eabon, and many more I can't remember.

About 4 PM that day, a single plane attacked USS *Phillips* and was taken under fire by all our guns. After the plane dropped three bombs, it passed up our starboard side at about 10,000 yards; a friendly fighter confirmed later that it was shot down. Our machine guns got the credit. This was the second plane we destroyed. Shortly after that, three planes flying over the beachhead came under fire from *Saufley*. We shot down two more, bringing our total to four that day. During all this time, we were laying smokescreens to cover the landing craft, which made the shooting more difficult. The brief description of this action only covers the shooting. We had been at General Quarters or Modified General Quarters for so long, it was like being physically beaten or totally drunk. No matter how tired you were, the sound of gunfire brought you completely awake.

On August 22, *Saufley*, *Renshaw*, and *Cony* were up the "Slot" to intercept the Tokyo Express. Early on the morning of August 23, with enemy planes all around us, *Saufley* was leading a column that came under attack by torpedo planes. We avoided one torpedo by emergency backdown, that is putting the ship's engine into reverse and maneuvering. Shortly thereafter, another torpedo passed 60 feet behind us. During this time, I was on the lower level of the forward engine room when I looked up at the man on the earphones, who was motioning me to come to the top of the ladder. We were at high speed and radical maneuvering and had been told to stand by for a torpedo. When it missed, I knew by the upper-level men's faces. I went to the main condenser, leaned against it, and got sick as a drunken man. I was sitting on my clothes bucket when Chief Curley banged a wrench for me to come to the top of the ladder. He said we had just had another torpedo pass to the stern and to remain alert in case of a hit. Everything had to be checked and reported in a hurry under these conditions. On that day, I earned my pay of $3.00, no doubt about it.

During all this action, the cooks served sandwiches with coffee to all hands. The reason we ate at battle stations was pure and simple—survival. Since most of the cooks and bakers had battle stations, only a few were left for galley work. Messengers would draw rations and bring them back for all men at battle stations. If someone had to go to the head, he would be relieved by the messenger. Sometimes, the chief on duty would release us so we could go topside to see the fighting or get some release from the close, hemmed-in feeling of the hot engine room during a fight. Chiefs Curley and Hastings were good about this and took their time going topside also. Chief Hastings had just made his rating and was an example to all the younger sailors.

We had our own coffeepots going in the engine room, and we also had rations delivered to the night watch. Usually, these rations were Spam, bread, bologna, or salmon. We called the bologna "horsecock." It came in big, round pieces a foot or more in length, sliced, and made into good sandwiches. We called the salmon "sea chicken" and the Spam "crap." We never liked the ones who sent us Spam.

Following our action of August 1943, *Saufley* was assigned to barge-hunting missions. On one night, our task force sank 24 barges, which were from 50 feet to 75 feet long. These barges were being used to transport troops with no escort. It was like shooting fish in a barrel, except they shot back with machine guns and rifles. The return fire did no harm. On another night, Squadron 22 sunk nine or ten barges off New Georgia Island. Later that night, when we were under orders not to fire at single planes, a near-miss killed Dr. C. R. Huffman and Store Keeper First Class Wyatt B. Wood and injured 11 men when it penetrated the hull in 20 or 30 places. Wood died that night and was buried in the military cemetery at

Guadalcanal. Dr. Huffman had a small piece of steel in his heart and died when he was sent to the rear at New Caledonia. Dr. Huffman had spent the whole afternoon on the fantail with the ship's crew checking the ones with the "thousand-yard stare." The doctor could send you home if he determined you were sick enough. He sat on the life raft and talked to me for a while. I had a premonition then that something bad was going to happen to him. I had this same premonition on two more occasions; I hope I never have it again.

When you have been underway and in battle for a week or so with only enough time to take on ammunition, food, and fuel oil, you get very tired and worn out. You are prone to forget everything, except the companionship of a woman, sleep, food, the beauty of a sunset or a sunrise, your hatred of the enemy, or the good earthy smell of the farm. Most of all at these times, I would remember my mother's love when I was young. She would rub my hair in her own loving way and make trouble go away. A mother always goes to war with her son, even if she is physically half a world away.

⚓ 9 ⚓

WE ALL HAD A THOUSAND-YARD STARE

DECEMBER 1943 – AUGUST 1944

December 1943 and January 1944 found Saufley *performing escort duties for the reinforcement of Bougainville. In February,* Saufley *was engaged in the assault on the Green Islands which broke the Japanese Rabaul-Buka supply line and provided the Allies with another airfield near Rabaul. Antisubmarine patrols were followed by call fire support missions during the occupation of Emirau Island. This action, which completed the "ring around Rabaul", took* Saufley *into April. She had returned to the Emirau-Massau area when, on the morning of the 7th, she gained contact on a submerged submarine. Forty-five minutes and 18 depth charges later, two underwater explosions were heard. Within hours, oil covered the area. Postwar review of Japanese records identified the sunken submarine as I-2. Following escort duties to the Admiralties,* Saufley *returned to Purvis Bay on the 18th whence she conducted exercises with TF 38 into May.*

On 4 May, the destroyer sailed for Pearl Harbor. Arriving on the 12th, she sailed west again on 1 June as a unit of Task Force 51.18, the reserve force for Operation "Forager", the conquest of the Marianas. On D-day plus 1, 16 June, Saufley *and the other escorts shepherded their charges into the transport unloading area west of Saipan. Saufley was then reassigned to call fire support duties. For the next month, she continued call fire support screening, and shore bombardment operations in the Saipan-Tinian area. On 20 July,* Saufley *moved south for the invasion of Guam. Here, the destroyer provided call fire*

*support for the assault troops. She returned to Tinian on the 23rd
and supported the landings there on the 24th. For the next week, she
provided gunfire support and served on radar picket duty.*
    —*from* The Dictionary of American Naval Fighting Ships

Commander Dale Cochran,
assigned as our new commanding officer on December 6, 1943,
was without peer when it came to maneuvering and fighting a
destroyer. He was with us until 1945; the strain of continuous
wartime responsibility aged him in a hurry. We were lucky to
have retained him as we found out in the near future. When
we were underway, he would tell us over the loudspeaker where
we were going. He said every man aboard the ship counted
and that he depended on us to help bring the ship back. We
did.

The change of command from Captain Brown to Captain
Cochran was the smoothest change of command that ever
occurred. Commander Brown left and Commander Cochran
took over. They had worked as a team for so long that all we
had to do was continue doing our same duties but under a
different man. They were as different as sand and water, but
their basic policy was the same: "Win! We will do it together!"

It was clear to us that Captain Brown with his clear and
awesome presence was born to be an officer. Men respected
and trusted him. He was a leader. Later on at Okinawa, he was
Commander of Destroyer Division 122 on the picket line when
the suiciders came.

Between December 12 and 19, 1943, we had our second
seven days of liberty in Sydney for a total of 14 days of liberty
since we had joined the South Pacific Fleet at Guadalcanal on
December 8, 1942. During this second time at Sydney, the
seaman back aft of the engineering quarters had a girl aboard.
Both Fagan and I thought we heard a girl giggle two or three
times. Krieger, the Boatswain, wouldn't talk to us about it and
said we were crazy. Fagan wanted us to get a girl and take her

back to the Solomons. We got drunk and forgot to do it. We wondered later what Captain Cochran would have thought of that?

In Sydney, I stopped on the way back to the ship at a pub where many veterans of the Australian 7th and 9th Divisions were drinking beer. One of them was drunk and wanted a beer so I bought him one. Next, he wanted me to give him some money and, when I refused, he tried to fight me. When he went down and was laying on the deck, the other men gathered around and yelled, "Give him the boot, Yank! Give him the boot!" If our positions had been reversed, I hate to think what could have happened. They were good men to have on our side.

After Sydney, we went back to the Solomons. By late 1943 and early 1944, the Japanese were reluctant to fight. We had whipped their best, and the war was changing. We were now on the offensive, and they were on the defensive and would never again be a winner. Furthermore, they were losing their taste for battle.

Our torpedo boats would leave late in the afternoon and head up the "Slot." They had lots of area to cover and did it well. The destroyers took on fuel and ammunition in the daytime and hunted targets to lay it on at night. We were jealous when other ships got into action and we were not included. To a man, we were tired and bone-weary, yet everyone had one thought: "Win this damn war any way we could." Savo Island was the scene of much of our fighting at this time. The battleships and cruisers would move in and bloody each other well. The ones left would haul out to sea or back to Rabaul.

When we got close to Christmas in 1943, everyone was feeling as low as a snake's belly. We were upset when our supply ship was sunk. We were eating hardtack and had no cigarettes for the smokers. We were unhappy as hell at the prospect of not having turkey for dinner. Standing around in small groups and bitching about anything we could think of, we talked of home, baked ham and turkey, dressing, gravy, fresh rolls, sweet potato pies, pumpkin and mincemeat pies,

Liberty on George St. in Sidney, Australia, as tension visibly fades. Note the socially correct pinkie. Pictured at top, F1c James Fagan. Lower photo from left, GM3 John Cotter with friend from above.

cakes, candy, and our loving families. All of a sudden, word came from the radio shack—our Christmas dinner would be delivered on time. Our feelings did an about-face, and we had one of the best Christmas dinners I have ever had! I know it may sound childish, but we were like a new crew after Christmas that year.

The midnight to 4 AM watch on December 31, 1943, included John Larned, Art Larson, Foss, and "Skinhead" Deal. Shortly after watch started, Eddie Czechowski came up in the darkness to deliver a container of the worst coffee anyone had ever tasted. Since it was New Year's Eve, the four enlisted men chipped in $1.00 each and talked Eddie into using his key to the storeroom to steal a #10 can of peaches. In about an hour, Eddie came back, having done everything in total darkness. After we fought the top of the can with a screwdriver and pliers, the peaches turned out to be prunes! Everyone cussed that "dumb Polack" for a while, then ate the prunes. (Forty years later, Eddie attended his first reunion and Larned jumped him about the peaches. At Eddie's next reunion four years later, he finally delivered a delicious can of peaches, which he and Larned shared.)

On February 14 and 15, 1944, we acted as an escort to Bougainville landings and then went right on to the Green Island beachhead. We were attacked by several formations of enemy planes, but no damage was done. On February 29 and March 1, we bombarded the Cape St. George radar station, New Ireland, which was near that dreaded Japanese naval base at Rabaul. We also silenced batteries at Namatanai Air Field and several batteries at other bases. The night of February 29 was my hardest night at sea. I had such a bad feeling about the action that night, which never occurred before or after any other battle. I am damn glad such feelings didn't happen again as they could make a coward of a man in short order.

A dead body in the water can be most disturbing: arms and legs gone, head torn away, or any of the things men can do to render death, along with bites from sharks and barracuda. During these days of our offensive, Captain Cochran wanted

any bodies we found to be searched. Seaman First Class Czechowski was the bow hook man. A bow hook is a long, sturdy
pole with a semi-sharp hook pointed on the end that allows the
bow hook man to pull the boat to the dock or push it away. It
is very effective. Every whaleboat has one. Czechowski hooked
a corpse that was missing his legs and whose body was grossly
swollen. Dr. Jones ordered him to pull it to the boat. He did
and held the body to the boat while the doctor searched it in
the semi-rough seas. When the search was over, Doc Jones told
him, "Push it away; hurry, push it away." When Czechowski
pushed with the bow hook, he penetrated the stomach. The
erupting gas blew back and made everyone sick. They obtained
no intelligence from this search.

From March 11 to March 16, 1944, we bombarded Japanese
positions at Empress Augusta Bay, Bougainville Island, using
our 5-inch 38s, 20-mm, and 40-mm guns. While the PT boats
worked close ashore, we worked over their heads. Our feelings
ran deeply against our opponents, whom we called "Tigers of
Malay," "Butchers of Hong Kong," "Keepers of Bataan Death
March," "Conquerors of Corregidor," "Bombers of Pearl Harbor," "Sons of Heavens," and "Sons of Bitches." At this time,
we knew they were about to have hell melted and poured in
their pockets. *Saufley* sank another Japanese submarine on
April 7, 1944, near Emeru Island. Lieutenant Commander
Kazuo Yamaguchi of the Imperial Japanese Navy was in command on a supply trip to Rabaul. After establishing a sonar
contact, we dropped 18 depth charges over a 23-hour period,
and we heard and felt two underwater explosions. We saw a
diesel oil slick three-fourths of a mile by fourteen miles long.
The assessment was that we had insufficient evidence to claim
a kill. After the war was over, the Navy established that we had
indeed sunk this submarine and we were so notified.

Sinking the submarine was our last major action in the
Solomons. The Solomon campaign was over, and we were leaving forever. Twenty-three U.S. destroyers lay rotting at the
bottom of the sea. Out of a total of 52 destroyers lost in the
Pacific War, nearly one-half of them went down during the

Solomons' campaign. All of us who had been in the pre-war Navy knew some of the men who were lost and, to this day, at any meeting we are inclined to get emotional at the thought of so many good ships and men based in these faraway waters. In spite of these losses, we can all take comfort in the fact that we had met the enemy under adverse conditions and prevailed when it seemed that only he could win. We never gave up and, in the process, smote him all about his head, shoulders, hips, thighs, and shin-bones. When he pulled out, he learned the taste of defeat in leaving. From now on, he would be force-fed.

I'll never forget the time someone working in the bilges left several small deck plates loose. They should have been screwed to the metal angles that held them up. We were at Modified General Quarters (one half of the crew on station, the other half resting). All of a sudden, we heard the boom, boom of underwater explosions. The deck plates jumped and landed at crazy angles. The main engines revved up, and the turbines screamed. A messenger boy dropped a pitcher of cold scuttlebutt water from the top of the ladder at the portside entrance to the engine room above me. This caused me to become extremely angry at the one who left the deck plates loose and almost caused skid marks in my skivvies. My dear friend, Wynter Rogers, who dropped the water, and the upper-level men never even dreamed how close old Jernigan came to ruining his pants.

As we left the Solomons, I remembered "Pistol Pete," a gunner hidden in the hills, and how we tried to get him with counter-battery fire. He would fire from the hills and fade away. I also thought of "Washing Machine Charlie," a Japanese pilot who flew over at dusk regularly as clockwork. I wonder whatever happened to them.

Beautiful Tulagi, our anchorage, was a PT base; a destroyer, supply ship, and tanker anchorage; and a repair base for battle-damaged ships. Sailors were transferred stateside from here and new recruits came on board, some of them just in the Navy eight weeks. They learned in a hell of a hurry, for the fear of not knowing speeded up the learning process.

While we were in the Solomons, I met Caesar Romero on a tanker from which we took fuel. He was an enlisted man and as a Mexican-American, it was the best he could expect in those days. Most of the other movie stars entertained troops or got a soft spot in a stateside berth. We sure as hell never met Ronald Reagan or John Wayne. If they had fought as a team, the Japanese might have surrendered sooner and we could have gone home.

The list of destroyers lost in the Solomons reads as follows: *Aaron Ward*, air attack; *Barton*, surface action; *Benham*, surface action; *Blue*, surface action; *Brownsen*, air attack; *Chevalier*, surface action; *Cushing*, surface action; *DeHaven*, air attack; *Duncan*, surface action; *Edsall*, surface action; *Gwin*, surface action; *Henley*, submarine; *Jarvis*, air attack; *Laffey*, surface action; *Meredith*, air attack; *Monssen*, surface action; *O'Brien*, submarine; *Perkins*, collision; *Porter*, submarine; *Preston*, surface action; *Simms*, air attack; *Strong*, submarine; *Tucker*, mines; and *Walke*, surface action.

The honor roll of sunken destroyers in the Solomons area includes everything from old four-pipers to the new, 2050-ton Fletcher-class destroyers. All of these ships performed grandly. Many of them were sunk before the new paint had worn off the ships' bottoms. Most were sunk because they didn't have the correct ratio of trained men to untrained men, a problem the Navy had when trying to put a two-ocean Navy together on a moment's notice. The Japanese had trained their fleet in the art of night fighting. They prevailed during night fights until we got radar and learned to use it. When our people mastered night fighting, we started to win. There was no way we could fight well at night if we didn't have the training and equipment.

By 1944, we had been in action almost continuously in the Solomons for 22 months. The strain took its toll on each one of us in a different way. One day, I was sitting on a locker top when one of the petty officers walked up, hit me, and almost knocked me out. As he leaned over me, I grabbed his hair, put my sheath knife to his throat, and watched his eyes grow. When

I felt better, I gave the knife to Charlie Baum and we had a good spine-tingling fight. After the fight, this petty officer went running up and told the captain about it. Captain Cochran had us to Mast and busted us. I went to machinist's mate third class from machinist's mate second class and he was busted from water tender first class to water tender second class. I didn't realize how much the strain of command had told on Captain Cochran until he sent for me later to come to his cabin. He looked ten years older than he looked when I came aboard. He said, "Jernigan, the war is going to last a long time. You've been in a lot of it. If you keep on messing up, you're going to be ranking mess cook in the Navy and you know enough to be first class or chief." I acknowledged that I had been in a lot of trouble and was sorry, but there wasn't any way that I could keep from slipping up occasionally. I didn't plan on staying in the Navy anyway.

When we were new at the game of war, you hardly ever heard a cuss word in normal talk. Yet somewhere in the process of becoming warriors, cussing at all things and people became normal. Each man's face and actions changed with his words. Everyone had decided to die if the gods of war called his name. We had changed from humans to brutal savages. As the months turned to years, our hatred for the Japanese was ever on our minds like a festering sore that we could never fully rid ourselves of in this life. New men arriving from the states were shocked at our attitude, but they changed too after a while.

Many times, men would get mad with one another, go to the fantail, put on the gloves, and fight like all get-out until one of them won or both got too tired to continue. Then they would throw their arms around each other and quit, friends forever.

As we departed the Solomons, the Navy was breaking up the best group of ships' officers and men, equal to any the world will ever produce. Destroyer Squadron 22 had a ball and chain for an emblem showing we had been assigned to the Solomons and forgotten. *Saufley*'s Captains Brown and Cochran were as good as any the Navy could produce. Still, *Saufley* had never been in a surface action against Japanese ships, and it gave us a bitter taste not to have seen action in a bang-up surface battle. This feeling still lurks in the recesses of my mind as a part of our job not completed, kind of like going to the Super Bowl and not playing.

The pre-war Navy was thinking of ship-to-ship fighting with torpedoes and main battery guns. *Saufley's* crew was good as any ship could expect to be. We could sink a floating barrel at five miles. Why, we asked, didn't the gods of war give us just one good surface-to-surface fight against the enemy? We had met and whipped him on many occasions and wanted to sink a Japanese "man-o'-war" of any kind. We had never been written up for our fighting ability. We were plainly jealous of other ships that had been given unit citations and various awards, although we had accomplished the same thing, as good or better.

Nick DeSimone was a young sailor on our ship and very much impressed with the fact that you could get hurt. He told me once that during our first air attack, Chief R. H. Thompson told him to check the bearing temperatures all around just to help him get rid of the "flutter willies." Nick was still showing his fear at the time. He looked across the main engines at old Chief Thompson, who had pulled out his false teeth and was holding them up clicking them at him, indicating that his bite was worse than the Japanese. Nick laughed and learned to control his fear at the same time. He said later that he was topside close to number 5 gun when we had a near-miss. He turned his back to the explosion and felt something hot in his pants. A small piece of hot steel had penetrated his pants and burned him.

Underway from the Solomons, we proceeded at a fuel-saving pace on a zig-zag course across the Pacific. We had ideas of going to Pearl Harbor, fueling up, and heading for the States to get fixed up because we were worn out. The scuttlebutt had it we were going to San Francisco or San Diego and that we were going to get repaired or take the ship back and leave it in dry dock and bring another one out. All kinds of scuttlebutt

was going through the ship at once. We proceeded all right —
straight to Pearl Harbor and around to Ford Island where we
tied up and took on fuel, ammunition, and supplies in a hell
of a hurry.

As Diamond Head came into view, it hit each of us in the
gut just as if December 7th had happened yesterday. The same
hills and submarine nets, but new commanding officers and a
more wide-awake defense. Guns were manned in the hills;
planes and radar were ready for combat. Officers listened to the
men who manned them.

When seeing Pearl City, it struck me that many men died
without knowing what happened and they were not ready to
meet their Maker. Many were at church or getting ready for
church as gleeful Japanese did their best to kill everyone in a
surprise attack. Some were blown to bits by direct hits. Concussion killed some, and many died slowly as the air was used
up in flooded compartments. Some gave up and drowned in
the rising water. No one in the Fleet has ever forgotten these
men. The *Arizona* Memorial at Pearl Harbor is a permanent
reminder that we should never again assume we are safe. May
the good Lord look with kindness on these men who gave their
lives and the family of states they represented.

We were in such a hurry to get back into action that we
were barely able to take on the fuel, ammunition, and supplies
we so desperately needed. We left in less than 24 hours with
the Northern Attack Force on June 1, 1944. Outside of Kwajalein anchorage, we had a submarine contact on June 11 and
conducted depth charge attacks until we were relieved by the
USS *Franks*. When we left, the oil slick was 3000 yards long
by 1600 yards wide. We pulled alongside a tanker with an
Indian crew who spoke English with an accent. Fagan and I
made a deal for a bottle of whiskey for $35.00 each. Captain
Cochran noticed Fagan and me making the deal and yelled
down to the oil king to get us away from the crew of the other
ship! He was too late. I can't figure why he didn't trust us
ashore or around strangers.

Saufley arrived in Saipan on June 16 and covered the landing of reinforcements during the period from June 1 to August 8, 1944. We engaged in 23 shore bombardments and 10 star shell missions while shooting 4000 rounds of 5-inch 38 shells, 400 star shells, and thousands of 20-mms and 40-mms as well. The number of assignments alone shows how well we got on target. We neutralized enemy troop concentrations; sank a corvette and several small craft; and destroyed runways, several buildings, a plane on the airfield, an ammunition dump, and gun emplacements. We also harassed Tinian Town and several groups of enemy troops on Tinian.

Saufley worked in close to the shore with assigned targets in the same way that the PT boats had worked with us at Empress Augusta Bay. The firing went on all hours of the day and night. With targets visible everywhere, we had a chance to see what we were accomplishing for the first time. It was good. We could see the Marines moving as if in broken order drill: forward, kneel, fire, move on. We could see flamethrowers, tanks, and individual Marines getting after the enemy. The Japanese called the Marines "devils in yellow leggings." We could smell the dead. Big, blue-tailed flies were everywhere, grown fat on human flesh. Bodies in the water floated by like strollers in Central Park on Sunday afternoon. The cruisers were in line behind us. Their shells came over our heads like freight trains with the fabled Casey Jones at the throttle. Like Casey Jones, they created one hell of a blast when they landed. At night, the tracers weaved intricate patterns in the sky and 14-inch, 8-inch, 6-inch, and 5-inch shells from the great battleships behind us each sang a different tune as they delivered their messages. They might come from the same gun, but each came with a different set of noises as they followed each other's slipstream. It was beautiful, yet solemn as a burial at sea.

During the period from June 16 through July 24, 1944, Lieutenant Martin, our gunnery officer, was so busy that he lost 20 pounds. I know that he was worried over the deaths of the women and children who were killed and wounded by the thousands.

Our days at Saipan consisted of laying to in the water and firing at specific targets designated by the Marines and the Army, firing at any planes that came in, keeping a look out for submarines, and trying to act normal. You couldn't act normal because there was shooting all day and night, and you couldn't sleep. The most often asked question was, "What did you say?" The guns going off had affected everyone's hearing. The damage lasts for some today. The worst thing about Saipan was the huge number of big, green flies. While eating a sandwich under the downdraft in the engine room, one man saw a fly come down the blower and land right on his sandwich. I think that was probably the end of his meals for that day.

Saufley was attacked by planes on June 17. We fired on two Tonys overhead but had no results. On the next day, we fired on three Tonys out of a group of twelve and chased them into several of our own fighters who shot down at least six of them. On June 19, one Zero took off from Tinian and attacked *Saufley*, but our machine gun fire drove him off. A Hellcat finally got him. I would like to think that we were their designated target because of the damage we were doing to them. On June 26, our main battery set fire to a Betty, but I'm not sure if he was shot down.

One day, we picked up two Japanese soldiers who had swum out to sea. Someone wanted them brought ashore. Our new men tried to act humanely to them, but most of the old hands would like to have seen them terminated. When a small Navy craft with two Marines came out to pick them up, they bowed down to the Marines. One Marine said, "You son of a bitch, if you try to escape before we get ashore, I'll shoot you right in the mouth, you bastard." Hell, some of us wanted to deep-six them right where they were.

On another day, we were 200 yards or more from the beach to the right of Grapan Town. Everything was in shambles along the beach with snipers still shooting at the Marines. When one sniper was flushed out, he tried to run across a wide, flat area with no place to hide. One of our fighter aircraft was strafing him. The bullets kicked up little, dusty footsteps that quickly caught him and kicked him into the heavenly realm the Emperor gods had made for him.

Much has been written about the dead at Saipan's Suicide Cliffs. The cliffs were on a high point at the north end of the island called Maripa Point. There were many hiding places along the cliffs for the military and civilian populations. If the entrance to the caves was in our line of fire, we could get to them. Otherwise, the Marines had to go in and mop up. I watched a Marine one day on a rock above some Japanese holed up in a cave. Our 20s and 40s were ineffective in this situation because of the angle of the cave's opening. The Marine tried dropping hand grenades, but they rolled downhill. Finally, he tied a rope to some explosives, swung it far out, and snatched it back into the cave. The Marines call this a satchel charge. I decided it was effective when he descended and fired into the opening.

Finally, Japanese soldiers and civilians started jumping from the cliffs into the sea and onto the rocks below. Whole families were killed or thrown over; some joined hands and jumped. High tides gathered the bodies from the rocks and swept them out to sea.

We were in close to Suicide Cliffs and could see the Japanese as they jumped to the rocks below. They also killed themselves with hand grenades, knives, or whatever was at hand. It would break your heart to watch. Whole families jumped and washed out with the tide. The hands and arms of the newly dead seemed to wave when they rose and fell with the waves. The girls' hair, all black and shining in the sun, made you think of home and of your sisters and brothers, and how the Japanese military would treat them if the situation were reversed. You remembered how their military had acted in China, Singapore, the Dutch East Indies, the Philippines, Wake Island, and Pearl Harbor as they made fun of the ones they were killing and flaunted the rules of the Geneva Convention.

After four or five days off Saipan, we could see ditches above Grapan Town, cut by the Seabees using bulldozers, filled with the dead and then covered over. The flies got bigger, and the dead smelled worse. We used DDT for the first time to kill the flies and found it very effective. The dead were a horror to see. Many were mothers and children, which gave one a foreboding feeling. Only God knows how many people died; I don't believe the Japanese even knew. In my heart, I felt sorry for the women and kids and hated the Japanese military more than ever. It was stupid of the Japanese not to surrender. As long as they were armed, they could kill; we had to go on showing no quarter until they surrendered. We stayed in this area until it was finally secured. We were at Modified General Quarters. In this way, half the crew could rest. We changed duty every four hours.

We left Saipan on July 19 and went to Guam where we screened the heavy units during the initial landings on Guam Island. By this time, our 5-inch shells were turning over and over in the air because the rifling in the 5-inch barrels was so worn down you couldn't see it. We couldn't shoot well with guns that had no rifling. Our shells must have sounded like a crippled turkey flying. The whole crew was nervous and ready for a rest at this point. Everything aboard ship was about worn out, and we weren't worth a damn in the battle zone.

On July 24, 1944, we went back to Tinian Island for the pre-invasion and subsequent bombardment during the occupation. Although we were still having our problems with the guns and couldn't hit our targets like we should, the powers that be didn't seem to know it.

While we were shelling Tinian Island, the Marines and Army with guns emplaced on Saipan joined us in the pre-invasion blast. You could see their shells leave and land, and hear the noise when they went overhead. It's a noise once heard, always remembered. Seeing shells from a battleship was also most impressive. Once past you, they could be seen all the way in if you were to one side of the flight path.

Our supply lines to the Marianas Islands were 5000 miles long before the Saipan invasion. When I was ashore at Ulithi, I saw we had rations and war materials stored high above my

USS Saufley *showing the grime of war and some near hits after firing over 4000 rounds of 5-inch ammunition.*

PHOTO, WILLIS NORMAN

head, covering many acres of ground. It was hard to believe. Looking at these massive amounts of supplies, I suddenly realized we could go to Tokyo and only divine power could stop us.

About the time we started to shell Tinian, word began to buzz around the ship that *Saufley* was going home. *Saufley* had had enough. The crew was going to get rest and recreation. We'd see girls. We'd get our ice cream. We could have all the steaks we wanted. All of these beautiful things would happen, and the ship would be in dry dock for more than six months. All the guns were to be replaced and new radar would be installed. We were going to have it made for at least half a year.

About this same time, one of our young seamen was caught in a homosexual act. He was not more than 17 or 18 years old. Sitting on his seabag on the port quarterdeck as we pulled into port, his head hung down and great sobs came from him like the noise a man makes with a severe throat wound. It was strange that the Navy only discharged the feminine half of this homosexual tryst. As I walked by, he turned his back. The boys in the deck division called him "Alice."

⚓ 10 ⚓

UNDER THE
BAY BRIDGE

AUGUST 1944 – NOVEMBER 1944

Remaining in the Marianas until 12 August, the destroyer than sailed for California, arriving at San Francisco with her squadron, Destroyer Squadron (DesRon) 22, at the end of the month. Overhaul took her into October. On the 26th, she again steamed west.
—*from* The Dictionary of American Naval Fighting Ships

S*aufley* left the Marianas operating area for Pearl Harbor on August 12, 1944. We nearly ran out of fuel in sight of Diamond Head. The fuel pumps kept losing suction, and we were smoking for all the world to see. Chief Knight said we would make it on the fumes, and we did. The ship was refueled and headed for San Francisco and dry dock at the Bethlehem Yard.

Since November 9, 1942, we had been at war continuously for over 20 months, logging close to 200,000 miles and defeating the enemy every time we came into contact with him. At the same time, we had trained and sent 200 new men back to the states to man new destroyers and had lost only two men to the enemy (Dr. Huffman and Store Keeper First Class W. B. Woods).

On August 31, 1944, after having been underway for 92 days except for fueling and taking on ammunition and stores,

Saufley had Navy yard availability for the next six weeks. The men of *Saufley* were to have port and starboard leave, liberty, girls, and whiskey for the next six weeks. It nearly killed me.

When we pulled into the ship channel and started under the Bay Bridge, it was a pretty sight with our bow wave rolling toward the beach so fast that small craft washed ashore. Captain Cochran had to explain to the yard commander why he came up the channel so fast when he was turning up so few revolutions on the cruising engine against an outgoing tide. With the city above us, every man was as nervous as a bird dog pup on his first point. My mouth was dry and my gut had "flutter-willies" like the ones I always got before a fight. When we went into the city, old San Francisco swallowed us like a big frog eating a fly. More than three hundred men walked off the ship and disappeared. I guess everyone found exactly what he wanted. I did. When we put to sea again, I had boozed it up so much and for so long that the nights were green instead of black. When I first walked on stable earth again, I found myself pausing in midstep to catch the roll of the ship and adjust my gait. The ship seemed all forlorn and lonesome with the crew in temporary quarters. I went back aboard and tried to sleep there, but I couldn't. The ship wasn't alive anymore, and you simply couldn't sleep on a dead ship.

On my first night ashore, I don't know how it happened. I went out the Navy yard gate and into the first bar on the right. That is the last thing I remember clearly. The rest of the night was a series of fights and encounters with Shore Patrol. One Shore Patrol officer beat me on the bottom of my shoes. I was thrown in the brig for fighting with a Marine, who was also locked up. Machinist's Mate Second Class Herman Burger saw the Shore Patrol lock me up and haul me away that night. He said I gave them a hard time. I must have put up one hell of a fight because, the next morning, three Shore Patrol with sidearms and a submachine gun returned me to the ship. For the life of me, I can't remember who it was, but one of the junior officers raised hell with the Shore Patrol and made them take the clip out of the tommy gun before I got on the gangplank. As I passed by, the Officer of the Deck said to the boatswain that the fight must have been something to see. They handed him papers on me. I never saw them again. I went ashore the next night, stayed sober, and had lots of fun. I think all the girls in town wanted a sailor from the destroyer fleet. The girls were good, bad, and indifferent; but they had one thought in common: find a sailor and mother him, get drunk, have fun, and get in bed. It was kind of like giving the condemned man a good meal before executing him. We couldn't get enough.

After one all-night stand, Chief Water Tender Jim Knight was almost to the main gate at Bethlehem Steel Yard at Hunter's Point. Truly drunk, he still had to get across the street and in the gate. His green, encrusted cap was pushed back, his tie was loosened around his neck, his eyes were red, and he needed a shave. Jim would stagger up to a building or light pole and hold it up with much effort. His coat with all the hash marks was buttoned at the top and his shirt was open to his belt. A Wave officer came out of nowhere, caught Jim at the light pole, and proceeded to give him a good Navy dressing-down. Jim held the light pole until it got steady again and told the Wave, "Sir, I know we have sailors like you in this man's Navy, but you are the first one I ever saw in a skirt!" He then left the pole on its own and staggered happily past me and George Duffy back home in *Saufley*.

We were too small to have a chaplain on board and usually didn't have a chance to go to services on a larger ship because of the urgency of wartime operations. Lieutenant Boyes was the officer of the deck when the assistant chaplain of the San Francisco area came aboard and asked to see the chaplain. As a joke, Boyes passed the word for Lieutenant Dan Michie to lay up to the wardroom where the assistant chaplain was waiting. Lieutenant Michie said the chaplain was a kind, elderly man who wanted to supply him with religious materials. Making a snap decision, Michie asked for Torahs, rosaries, Bibles, things for one Mormon and one Christian Scientist, and even a book by Mary Baker Eddy. The supplies came aboard in a few days. Later as we sailed under the Bay Bridge and out to sea, Lieutenant Michie put a message in our first newsletter that anyone wanting religious materials should see him. His supplies were exhausted in two days. The men started asking him when he would have religious hours. He found to his surprise that one of his duties was listed as the ship's chaplain. Gunner's Mate First Class John C. Klingensmith kept after Michie to have religious hours, until he scheduled them in his stateroom. He sat and listened to what the men said, which seemed to make them happy, but Klingensmith never came.

While still in San Francisco on September 15, 1944, I went home on 12 days of leave. My good old Texas shipmate got drunk with me in San Francisco, and we were in that same shape when we reached Houston, Texas. We were seated with two Waves who had been drinking with us on the train. My shipmate lived near Houston, and I had an overnight layover with a room booked at the Ben Milam Hotel.

As we were leaving the station at Houston, my Texas shipmate forgot he had a wife meeting him. He was walking with the Waves' assistance, one on each side, and I was following about ten feet behind. His little wife was there and hit him harder than the rooster hit the little red hen. The Waves ran! His wife proceeded to beat him a few more licks with her purse, grabbed his arm, straightened his neckerchief, and took him away. He never came back to the ship, and I never heard from him again.

From Houston, I rode a dirty train to New Orleans and then back to Chattahoochee, Florida, to see my family. The farther I went from *Saufley* and my family of shipmates, the more troubled I became. Although many of my shipmates had been transferred to other duties, the old-timers were still in *Saufley*. I missed them, every damn one, even the officers. I could not cast away the closeness we had built up among us.

Being home again was like a bad dream. My loving family was not the same I remembered from long ago. I loved them but felt we had nothing in common. We had never shared the harshness of days, nights, and endless months at war. They never knew the men I had laughed and talked with and the ships that had changed course, all going to that last anchorage located at the bottom of the many battle sites from Cape St. George, Bougainville, Blackett Straight, Vella Gulf, Choiseul, Kula Gulf, Savo, or Iron Bottom Sound. They had never experienced the feeling I had when one of my best friends went down in cruiser *Helena* on July 6, 1943, in the dark waters of Kula Gulf—the price one pays in war. One never forgets the face and name of lost shipmates. I came to realize how lonely I was and wished I was back in San Francisco with my shipmates. Only shipmates were important to me. You couldn't defile these cute little girls at home. There were no bars, no veterans to talk with, and no sailors. There were only young draftees in clean-pressed uniforms with hope eternal in their eyes and no money in their pockets. They offered drinks and wanted to talk. "How was it? Were you afraid? Where did you go?" After a while, I went to the roadhouse where I could buy some whiskey. A boy in uniform with a girl on his arm wanted to fight me there; he called me yellow when I wouldn't. I didn't want to fight him. Why did he dislike me? My friend, Frank Ellis, and someone else took him to the doctor.

I went home at 10:00 PM. Mom was sitting up sewing, just waiting to talk. Dad was at work at the power plant, and my brothers and sisters were asleep. I wanted to lay my head on Mom's knee and let her rub my troubles away, but big boys don't do that. So I went to bed. With only a few more days of leave left, I just wanted to return to San Francisco and get back with my shipmates. Why had I wanted to go home anyway? Home had changed; everyone was worried about ration coupons. It seemed that only food, clothes, and shoes were important to them. Jobs were foremost on their minds. It was as if a dark curtain was drawn between me and my family, and I could not penetrate it. I felt as if I was one of the four horsemen and they wanted to avoid me. I was sad and wanted my shipmates. Men went to sea. It was all like a dream.

When my leave was over, I caught a taxi by myself to River Junction, boarded the train, and sat in a crowded car with old people and new draftees. With layovers and slow trains, it took me four days to get to San Francisco. On the train, I met one lady in her early thirties who worked for the Red Cross. She was on her way home to Oakland, California, and was very troubled by her wartime experiences with used-up servicemen from the Anzio beachhead. We talked for hours. I was supposed to go see her at her house, but never made it. When I got to San Francisco, I joined the crew and enjoyed the rest of our stay very much. The Irisher Club and the Eddie Hotel at Eddie and Mason Streets were our hangouts until we got ready to go to sea again.

On October 18, 1944, it was time to get up steam, raise vacuum, and check everything out. When we were anchored in the bay again, we had our last look at a beautiful place. We looked at the city, hills, trees, flowers, cars, white houses in the distance, and girls who were fun to be with. We had to leave and get back to eating fried Spam, watered dehydrated eggs, and potatoes. We also had to face standing in chow lines and watching officers' eggs, ham, breakfast fruit, and steaks go by on trays carried by black or Filipino mess boys. They, too, were second class.

The captain's gig (boat) was an emblem of the ship, the captain, the crew, and the crew of the gig. It was kept as clean as a cook's oven at inspection time with white monkey fists and ropes of all kinds put together most painfully by the leading seaman and coxswain under the boatswain's glaring and watchful eye. The bell for signals was so shiny it hurt your eyes. When we were at anchor and other captains would visit, it was a sight to see. Each crew and captain thought they were the very best and would parade around like they were in a beauty contest. The one who lorded it over everyone else was "30-knot" Burke. His gig looked pretty as an Easter bonnet in a parade. The only thing that didn't shine was the gold braid on the officers' caps. They all seemed to want it to turn green and look old.

While we were still anchored at San Francisco, there came a joyous sound . . . liberty being announced. Someone said the liberty was only for married men. Newby, Fagan, and I couldn't believe this was happening since most of the veterans weren't married. Captain Cochran wouldn't do that. Newby went to see Captain Cochran to tell him we also want to go ashore. We watched men just out of boot camp already going ashore. Cochran told us to shut up and forget it or he'd have us locked up.

We weren't deterred, however. We slipped into our dress blues, went to the fantail, and took the Captain's gig. The man on gig duty even cast off for us. We were mad as hell by now. When we rounded the starboard side and started toward Fisherman's Wharf, Cochran was on the flying bridge with a loudspeaker. He wanted to blast us out of the water. The gun mounts swung around to us, but we steered a course that kept other ships in his line of fire. I guess Dale Eugene Cochran nearly had a heart attack that day.

We tied up at the wharf. Fagan and I went to the Irisher Club and Newby went to see his girlfriend. We got drunk and were having a good time when the shipmate, who had started the fight with me long ago and caused us both to be busted at Captain's Mast, showed up. He had been transferred after I had publicly humiliated him and I did the same that night. We went on to several other places, got drunker, and found more trouble. We finally got into a good, rib-busting fight with each other on the pier, fell into the bay, got out again, and caught a fleet runabout back to *Saufley*. Newby came aboard later.

Captain Cochran leaned over from the bridge when I came aboard and told someone to seize me and lock me up. I just went to my bunk and fell asleep. Fagan hid on top of the boiler in the fireroom. Newby went to his bunk when he came aboard. On the next morning around 10:00 AM, Cochran gave the boatswain mate a direct order, "Lock them up." Boatswain's Mate First Class Krieger woke Newby to say he would serve us all the whiskey we could drink if we would get up and go to the boatswain's locker forward and starboard. Newby called me with this news and so we went. Krieger didn't lock the door, and they couldn't find Fagan. Later, Cochran stuck his head in our little bar, and I cussed him out. We finally sobered up, let ourselves out, and went on watch. We were at sea again. Newby and Fagan were each busted one rate at Captain's Mast, but they never tried me.

When we went on to the San Diego destroyer base to take on ammunition, not one of the unmarried veterans would help. We were still mad as hell by then and would have fought an admiral over that stupid damn order. What happened really amounted to mutiny. It was a bad event that all of us wished had never happened, even the officers. Chief Jim Knight walked among us and asked us to forget it and load ammunition, which we finally did. A real bad incident was eventually cooled off. None of the officers ever mentioned it after this time. Again, we became a ship's crew ready to do battle with the Japanese, even letting the married men go to the fight with us.

Heading back into the Pacific on October 26, 1944, the waves played Russian roulette with us and savaged us in much the same way a cat plays with a bird before turning it over to his kittens. Each wave came in more savagely than its predecessor with a white cap perched on top foaming like a mad dog. If I looked up, I saw skies that scared hell out of me for they were the same color as the sea. If I went to the leeward side, I had to hold on for dear life while looking down at the swirling sea ready to suck me under. I looked up at the stacks and saw they were ready to swallow enough water to douse the fires in the boilers and cause them to blow. The bridge was empty; I could see no one at all. It seemed to me that I might not make it down the hatch and into the engine room; Elliott would have to stand watch forever. Yet here I was, holding onto a piece of steel, afraid to turn loose and afraid not to. I had seen battle and it was not like this. I had had my share of joy and seen much trouble, but right then I said, "O Lord, give me a sign." I started to count waves. I counted five waves; the fifth one was smooth. I'd count again. Number five was smooth again. But I still couldn't turn loose. I counted one more time. That time, the fifth one was so rough the expansion joints groaned like they were alive. I thought back to the time when Admiral Wilcox was swept from the deck in the Atlantic. Was he counting waves too? It didn't matter for he was old and couldn't move fast. One wave got him. It had a white cap on it too.

When I finally reached the engine room, they looked at me and laughed. The word had been passed that we were not to relieve the watch until it calmed down and a line could be tied up for us to hold as we worked our way across the deck. It was too rough topside that night for man or beast.

During heavy weather, your position in the ship dictated the type of *ride* you received. In the seaman's quarters near the bow during bad weather, the ship would groan like she was in labor. Her bow would get heavy sledgehammer blows as the breaking waves washed across the deck. A seaman in his bunk would roll to the bulkhead and back to the two tie chains that held the folding bunk in a horizontal position. Sometimes, when the bow descended back into the water, he would bump the bunk above. We remained dressed during this type of weather because of the constant movement. Sometimes we rode hundreds of feet on the crest of a wave before settling in again. Going into the engineers quarters, you had to grab anything nearby to stay in position for you had no footing. If you reached for a bunk and missed it, you would grab wildly at anything else in reach while bumping shipmates and trying to stay vertical. Sometimes you hit a slick spot where a shipmate had left his lunch and that just moved you along faster! The drive shaft from the engine to the propellers speeded up when the propellers were out of the water during rough weather, making our quarters come alive with vibrations. The noise drowned out some of the sound of the seas around us. The seamen aft of us had the same noises with a more pronounced up-and-down motion that made them feel like their stomachs were up in their throats.

The bridge was also in constant motion fore and aft, port to starboard, in a violent dance pushed by the wind and waves. Seamen grabbed anything handy to stabilize themselves, holding on so hard their hands turned white and bloodless. We were locked in a life-or-death fight with the sea with the outcome always in doubt. The helmsman had to fight to keep us on course, or we would lose headway and be swamped. The wind, waves, and rain sounded like banshees as the ship moved like a cork in a washing machine. Everyone had a queasy feeling in the stomach the entire time.

We never had a problem with men stealing from one another. Once in a while, however, a man new to the service had to be straightened out. There were several ways to do this. Sometimes a group of men in his division would do it, or a senior petty officer might talk to him.

I walked into the head one night as Boatswain's Mate First Class Krieger talked to one who had been stealing. The boy's eyes, nose, and mouth were bleeding. Krieger finished his talk just as I walked in. He said, "So help me God, you bastard, do that one more time and I'll feed you to the fish." The problem was solved. Stealing was just not allowed. We enlisted men had a handle on it and dished out swift, sure justice.

At one time during our duty in the South Pacific, I had just relieved the watch and was over on the port side under the electrical switchboard hunting for some canned sausage I had stashed on one of the horizontal hull support members. I was climbing up to get the sausages when I heard a noise like sandpaper on a screen wire. I laid my hand on the hull plate and could feel a slight shudder. Then it stopped. I was not alarmed and forgot it until I went topside later during the watch. The sea was calm and you could see where the water changed color all around the ship, indicating we were in a reef area. We were going very slowly and changing course heading into the shore. I walked forward to the bow and heard a call as old as sailing itself. The boatswain and two seamen were taking soundings with a lead line. The lead was something like an old-style window weight with wax in the end to pick up soil samples with color markers on the line. Each color would show you a different fathom mark. For example, if blue was 4 fathoms, a boatswain would call mark 4 and deeper or mark 4 and shallow. The call was relayed to the bridge by phone. It didn't take a genius to figure out that, if we were attacked, we could not maneuver here at all. We could only stand and fight. Luckily, no planes came and no shore batteries fired. We got out safely and I was back on watch when we cleared the reefs and speeded up.

What I saw on deck that day was a lesson in seamanship. I believe the boatswain was named Eckel. I can still see the seaman but can't remember their names. They would coil the line, holding part of it in one hand and the running part in their throwing hand. Then they would give the line several whirls and let it fly straight in front of the ship. It sank in a hurry and, when it stood straight down, they took the reading. The seamen who took soundings were usually senior seaman first class. They had to be good line men because, if they were slow, the ship would be aground. This situation represents one time that the boatswain and his seamen told the officer on the bridge what to do.

⚓ 11 ⚓

RISING SUN SETTING

NOVEMBER 1944 – NOVEMBER 1945

On 17 November, she arrived at Ulithi Atoll. Proceeding to Leyte Gulf, Saufley *soon found herself engaged in antisubmarine action after moving into the Camotes Sea to search for a submarine reported to be in the area. Shortly after entering the area on the 28th, the Japanese submarine was located on the surface off Pilar Point, Ponson Island. In a multi-destroyer gun action involving* Saufley, Renshaw *(DD-499), and* Waller *(DD-466), the submarine was sunk 45 minutes later.*

Returning to Leyte Gulf, Saufley *lost one man and suffered considerable hull damage in an engagement with enemy planes on the 29th. Following repairs at the Admiralties, she proceeded to a 2 January 1945 rendezvous with the Lingayan attack force. Moving into the Sulu Sea on the 7th,* Saufley *shot down an attacking Japanese aircraft at dusk on the 8th. On the morning of the 9th, the formation stood into Lingayen Gulf.* Saufley *provided screening services as the assault waves landed in the Lingayen area. On the morning of the 10th,* Saufley *splashed another aircraft, this time a Val attempting to crash the destroyer.* Saufley *got underway on the 12th to return to Leyte Gulf. From Leyte Gulf, she escorted a convoy to Morotai and returned on the 26th. Sailing for Luzon,* Saufley *arrived off Nasugbu to support the landing there on the 31st. On 1 February, she sank an attacking Japanese boat. She then commenced call fire support which continued for four days.* Saufley *then set a course for Subic Bay.*

The balance of February and most of March was spent in support operations in the areas of Manila Bay and Mindoro. Saufley *participated in amphibious operations at Sanga Sanga (31 March to 4 April) and Jolo (8 to 11 April) where she served as flagship, screening vessel, and call fire support ship.*

The next two months found Saufley *engaged in escort duties. She*

participated in the assault against Balikpapan, Borneo, on 1 July.
The destroyer returned to Morotai on 22 July. She engaged in escort
work between Leyte Gulf and Ulithi until the end of hostilities in mid-
August. —*from* The Dictionary of American Naval Fighting Ships

Saufley reported to the 7th Fleet Commander on November 17, 1944, at Leyte Gulf, Philippines, under operational command of General MacArthur. For the first time, *Saufley* had P-38 fighter planes instead of Navy or Marine planes. On November 22 and 24, we were under air attack, but there were no results. On November 27, I was topside when 12 to 15 planes attacked. Our main batteries shot one plane down and the machine guns cold-handed another one on the starboard side. We fired on a torpedo plane, which crashed without doing any damage to the ship. When we were in the Solomons, Japanese pilots complained about the 5-inch "machine guns." I guess our gunners had the right reputation for they were scoring on that day. You could tell by the look in their eyes and the way they walked.

On that same night, we went on a high-speed run around the tip of Leyte and right into Ormoc Bay. It was our first attack on Ormoc. The sweep was very successful and kept us on our toes all night. We fired 120 rounds of 5-inch shells on predetermined targets and many 40-mm and 20-mm shells. We then made a high-speed run out to sea only to get a submarine on the surface report from a PBY back in Ormoc Bay. The target, Japanese submarine I-41, commanded by Lieutenant Commander Fumitake Kondo, was picked up at six miles. *Renshaw*, *Waller*, and *Saufley* opened fire. We used both main batteries and machine guns. The submarine probably couldn't dive because it returned our fire with machine guns instead of diving, a foolish maneuver. When Chief Hastings sent me topside, I thought I saw the submarine sink; but there were so many shells landing, it was hard to see. Kondo and his whole crew were lost. This I-41 submarine had sunk a cargo ship and seriously damaged our light cruiser *Reno* earlier in the deployment.

On November 29, 1944, we were on patrol (later called a picket patrol), looking like fodder for the suicide planes. I was sleeping on an army cot about 30 feet from the entrance of the engine room on the port side when something woke me up. The first thing I saw that day was a plane with meatballs on the wings just rolling into a dive. The General Quarters alarm was going, the machine guns were firing, and everyone was running to their battle stations. I swung my feet off the cot and started to run to my engine room battle station, but someone had tied my shoe strings together as a joke. I hit that steel deck flat on my stomach and kicked my feet to break the shoestrings. People were running fore and aft all over me. I don't know how I did it, but before the plane hit, I was in the engine room. All of this time we were gaining speed and turning hard left to avoid the plane. All the guns were firing when the Japanese plane hit, crashing close to the starboard side forward and causing much damage. We stopped all engines and were checking for leaks and damage to the steam lines and pumps when we went to flank speed again, turning hard right with all guns blasting. A second Japanese plane appeared on the port side and, once again, our gunners put the cold hand on the plane, causing it to crash portside and inflicting some damage. When the plane hit, Machinist's Mate First Class Robert E. Lee Jones was up close, looking right at the pilot. Something mushy was on Jones' forehead as he ran around to the starboard side. Dr. Jones came out of the wardroom door and grabbed Jones, thinking he was seriously wounded. On closer examination, it was the pilot's brains and not Robert E. Lee Jones, who was injured only slightly by a cut caused by a piece of the Japanese pilot's skull.

Following this action, things got quiet again. Once more we started checking for damage when the guns began to fire. We were in a high-speed hard left turn when another Japanese plane flew between our stacks and released its bomb load, exploding close to the starboard and injuring more people. We lost one shipmate over the side; 26 others were injured, none seriously. Steward's Mate Second Class Evan Allen was the one lost as a result of this attack. No one knows exactly what happened to him, but I think he was blown over the side by one of the three Japanese planes. The injured were Lieutenant (jg) Raymond W. Allen, Lieutenant (jg) John L. Boyes, Machinist Douglas R. Smith, Seaman First Class Alfonso B. Alarid, Fireman First Class Lewis F. Bailey, Gunner's Mate Third Class Arthur Cyr, Coxswain George W. Dace, Ship's Cook Second Class Frank T. Daloia, Yeoman Third Class Joseph F. Devine, Seaman First Class James A. DiBenedetto, Seaman First Class Maury G. Donato, Fireman First Class Albert J. Dougher, Gunner's Mate Third Class James Duprey, Seaman First Class Anthony J. Eabon, Machinist's Mate Third Class Joseph Englehardt, Coxswain Edward N. Horn, Machinist's Mate First Class Robert (E L) Jones, Seaman First Class Ernest F. Lee, Seaman First Class Lloyd L. Lyon, Seaman Second Class C. H. McCullough, Seaman Second Class Andy L. Parker, Seaman First Class Lloyd C. Phipps, Seaman Second Class Anthony B. Pizzo, Machinist's Mate First Class Robert H. Swan, Seaman Second Class Carl (G) Watts, and Seaman First Class James H. Wilson.

Another undocumented loss also occurred. Earlier at Nasugbu, Don Hastings brought a puppy aboard. The dog was hungry and dirty, but love and good food made him happy and fat. His coat of black and yellow spots was smooth as silk, and everyone loved him. On this day, with planes hitting close aboard in an air attack, no one thought of our pup. When it was over, he was gone.

Our ship sustained much damage on the starboard side of the bow just below the water line. There was some other damage on the port side main deck and up to below the bridge. Once again, I believe our mantle of luck was with us. At the same time we were hit, *Aulick* was attacked by other suicide planes, which left 32 dead and 64 wounded with most of the damage done to her superstructure. She continued patrolling until relieved by *Pringle*. *Saufley* remained on the patrol. Captain Cochran's quick decision and strategic actions should be credited with saving the ship.

We were finally sent to Ulithi to repair our battle damage. Mr. Swanson was a troubleshooter for General Electric in charge of our steam turbines until the Navy accepted them as ". . . in place and working to Navy specifications." He was as valuable to the Navy as any admiral and one of the best teachers for the machinist's mates. He would spend time with anyone who wanted to know about the turbines. His one great desire was to be in a sea battle. All of us liked him and his knowledge. I worked with him on both *Washington* and *Saufley* but had not seen him since *Saufley* was in the Brooklyn Navy Yard. In November 1944, we were at Ulithi harbor repairing battle damage. I was coming from the engine room heading aft to our washroom when a vaguely familiar voice behind me yelled, "Jernigan!" As I turned, Swanson was on me with a great bear hug, telling me he had seen an ammunition ship blow up and sink. He had come to check on our battle damage to decide if it could be repaired at Ulithi or be forced to go home. We had damage to frame 56 where one of the suicide planes had hit close to the ship, springing the frame and bending the hull plates. We didn't go home, and I never laid eyes on him again.

While at Ulithi to repair battle damage on the starboard side forward, every man aboard was busy working on the ship's bottom. While we were in a floating dry dock, each division had an area to chip and paint. In less than three days we did a week's work. Even the chiefs gave a hand. The seamen used chipping hammers and wire brushes as if they were being paid by the number of brushes they wore out. It was chip, wire brush, paint with red lead, and then paint with battleship gray. When we were at anchor, seamen went over the side in boatswains' chairs to chip, wire brush, red lead, and paint. We must have removed at least 25 tons of barnacles, which cut down on our speed. Everyone seemed to be proud of the chance to help.

Returning to battle, we had just beat off a heavy air attack and were making a run down the starboard side of a troopship

CMM Donald Hastings with ship's pup, Princess, in happier times.

PHOTO, WILLIS NORMAN

loaded with Army nurses. They all ran to the rail and were waving to us. How pretty they were! Each man thought they were only for him. Then we noticed they were pointing to our range finder where we had painted battle flags listing all the actions we had been in. All our egos deflated in short order. We thought we were just like the old western gunmen: lots of notches but no girls.

On December 2, 1944, three American destroyers made a sweep of Ormoc Bay. (They left USS *Cooper* on the bottom.) That same day, *Saufley* left for Manus Island to repair our battle damage. We were in a floating dry dock for three days.

The campaign in the Philippines was turning out to be the fastest and least costly of all our campaigns. With the loss of four of our destroyers at Ormoc Bay, a troop-staging area for the Japanese infantry had been turned into a defenseless beach where parts of our 77th Division marched ashore and met little resistance.

During our campaign in the Philippines, battleship *Maryland* was hit by a torpedo and we were assigned to move Admiral T.D. Ruddock's staff off the battleship. I was off-watch on the torpedo deck, but I observed every move as we went alongside, tied up, and piped the admiral and his staff aboard. Everything was precise and business-like, and I observed all these goings-on with great pride. I don't know who was the most grateful—the admiral or his staff, but they were very happy when they came aboard. I was also on watch when they left. Admiral Ruddock sent us a well-done message after the transfer.

As the war wound down, I became more and more aware of being away from my loved ones. Most of all, I wanted to be close to Mom and Dad and my two sisters and brothers. For the first time, I realized how much I wanted the intimacy of home and family and the loving touch of a girl friend. Mom had been a hugger, and the rest of the family was just as loving. I started to wonder if the wall between us would ever be removed. One question was always foremost in my mind: Would I ever again adjust to life as it had been before December 7, 1941?

We were in full contact with the enemy at all times around Christmas of 1944; yet, this holiday was one of our best since we were whipping the enemy every time we met him. The Japanese were reduced to suicide tactics at sea, in the air, and on the ground. Japan itself was also being bombed to rubble daily by our B-29 bombers in ever-increasing numbers. Whole Japanese armies were stripped of their honor as they died most painfully; their generals and admirals self-destructed as their fighting men sought death in final charges. Many Japanese civilians wanted the fighting to end; yet, they were powerless to stop the war until the Emperor told the military fanatics it was over. The atomic bomb was the clincher that finally ended their glory days.

We sailed alone to Hollandia in New Guinea on January 1, 1945, where we picked up intelligence photographs and joined the Lingayen attack forces. On the way to Lingayen Gulf on January 8, 1945, our convoy was attacked by eight planes that were later shot down by Army planes. One Val on our port side came under fire by all batteries. He went into a high-speed dive and circled our stern at an angle. At that point, we had to cease fire to keep from hitting our transports. The Japanese plane crashed astern of the nearest transport. Both *Saufley* and the transports had been firing at the plane, but we were given a sure assist in shooting it down because of our heavier, more accurate fire.

On January 6, 1945, starting at 11:00 AM in Lingayen Gulf and ending at 5:34 PM, a total of 32 Japanese suicide planes made contact with our force. The totals were: 12 hit the ships they dove on, 7 were near misses, and 13 were either shot down or crashed without doing any damage. These suicide planes or kamikazes were demoralizing to our fleet that was one of the largest ever assembled and staffed by many officers and men who had never heard a shot fired in anger. When we went into the Philippine waters, we expected the usual air attacks. We were accustomed to the Japanese idea, "No surrender, only death with honor." We knew how the Japanese civilians committed mass suicide at Saipan—babies, girls, boys, men, and women. These people were afraid to die, yet they were so frightened they did not want to live. In their last seconds on earth, these dedicated Japanese did tap dances through our anti-aircraft fire and maneuvered for position to try to harm us fatally. I believe our 20-mm and 40-mm guns did the most damage to their planes. At long range, it was the 5-inch 38 shells with proximity fuses set to explode near the plane. Speed and well-timed maneuvers were our best protection from their suicide missions. I imagine a suicide dive was like shooting fish in the water: something one had to learn to do. The suicide pilot had only one chance to do it in this world, which was a good thing for us. Actually, self-sacrifice is not illogical in the heat of battle; many of our Medal of Honor winners made that same sacrifice of self. Planned mass suicide, however, is not logical.

Once while we were at General Quarters after the first Japanese suicide planes started hitting our ships, I was sitting on my clothes bucket on the lower level of the engine room between checks of the main engine and pumps. A big pipe wrench, about 24 inches long, fell very noisily to the grating behind me and scared me half to death. Everyone on the upper level was looking real serious; there was no smiling or joking. When I went up and asked who had thrown the pipe wrench down, no one admitted it. I finally concluded that the wrench must have been left on one of the upper level beams in the engine room and just fell off.

Saufley participated in the invasion of the Lingayen Gulf, Luzon Island, on January 9, 1945. We screened the initial landings at Lingayen Gulf and, shortly afterwards, we fired on two planes. There were no results. Early on the morning of January 9, a Val came over our port bow, circled the ship, and made a suicide dive from the port beam. Our machine guns scored many hits that caused him to crash into the water close to the starboard. I had left the engine room to go to the head, and the Japanese plane crashed just as I walked out of the head. It gave me an eerie feeling to know that the pilot would actually kill himself to get me. Our people were all a bit nervous about this. Eabon would actually tell you that they were just after him and then he'd laugh. He was kind of crazy anyway and ready to fight at any time. His nose seemed to change positions from right to left each time he went ashore. You knew that this man would stick until the end when he was on the gun. Eabon was just an example of the many good men we had on every gun. Because he was close to the forward engine room, I could run forward and watch him in action when I got topside during a fight.

On January 12, *Saufley* fired at two Japanese planes but with no results. After departing Lingayen to Leyte Gulf as a screening ships for the transports, we picked up one survivor from a suicide crash on USS *Zeilin*. This man was so badly burned that his flesh was falling away. His face looked like an overcooked marshmallow that had turned black. One of our men who saw him later had a breakdown. We had worked with USS *Zeilin* in other places and felt this as a personal loss. After joining a convoy to Morotai and then back to Leyte Gulf, we escorted the Coast Guard cutter, *Ingram*, to the Subic Bay beachhead. We arrived on January 31 and proceeded to Nasugbu landing, acting again as a screening vessel. On February 1, 1945, we sank an attacking suicide boat loaded with explosives. Later that day, we laid the cold hand on a pocket of Japanese with the 5-inch gun. We then took eight Philippine soldiers, who had been wounded in an attack on a Japanese gun nest, to Mindoro. While attacking a machine gun nest, they had butchered the Japanese with bolo knives. Shot through the legs and hips and stil! on a battlefield high, the Philippinos were happy describing the attack like men on a drunk.

On February 12, 1945, Lieutenant Commander F. W. Silk relieved our Captain Dale Eugene Cochran. A sad day for us as Captain Cochran had continued the tradition of our beloved Captain Brown and was one of the best destroyer skippers in the U.S. Navy. The new Captain, Lieutenant Commander Silk, came from staff duty and was all spit and polish. He wanted us to muster every time we had an alert, and he wanted dress-white inspections instead of battle drills. Battle drills paid off but spit and polish made you tired. We had lost so much sleep that many of us just didn't go to inspections. When Silk left the ship once to go to a meeting, all the men topside cheered to see him go. Bursting with pride and thinking the cheers were for him, Silk raised both his hands above his head in a Churchill salute. I for one would have deep-sixed him quicker than a K-bar bites. Later, during the Vietnam War, I read of young soldiers fragging their officers. I wondered what kind of unfair treatment could cause this to happen, but then I knew when I remembered Silk.

In one case, after Commander Silk took command, he treated one of the black steward's mates so badly that the man often served wardroom coffee to that little tyrant with a generous portion of urine or spit. Even the other officers hated him and once had to stop one of their fellow officers from using a .45 gun on him. Captain Bligh of the *Bounty* was saintly compared to Silk.

Radioman Third Class George Duffy had the 4 AM to 8 AM watch and secretly typed orders for us to report to Pearl Harbor and San Francisco *immediately*! He went around while it was still dark and hung this order on all the bulletin boards. When the first shipmate read the order, he went to work telling everyone we were going home. We were talking about it in the chow line, slapping each other on the back, happy as five-year-olds in Santa's arms. Commander Silk heard about it at breakfast in the wardroom and yelled for his copy of the order. Soon afterwards, George was exposed and had to explain why he did it to Commander Silk.

On February 15, 1945, we helped with the invasion of Marvellas on Bataan Peninsula. *Saufley* worked the landings at Marvellas, Bataan, and Corregidor Island. We delivered counterbattery fire at Caballo while covering our minesweepers. That night, we fired at troops on the road leading to Marvellas. During the next day, *Saufley* covered the landing and paratroop jump on Corregidor. We were used to landing craft but not to paratroopers. It was a sight to see with our guns firing even as the paratroopers jumped! We bombed Corregidor until we wondered if it would sink into the sea. The island's green color quickly turned to brown. I just hoped that the Japanese who had occupied the island were still there to defend it.

On Corregidor and elsewhere, we destroyer men were proud of our ship and the service we were rendering our country. We had worked on the "Rock" long and hard, blasting away with the 5-inch guns, and the 20-mm and 40-mm guns as if our job was to destroy Corregidor itself. Our big horizontal bombers attacked the island aiming for the tunnels and everything else topside. Our small craft headed into the beach to add their own brand of torture. Surely the Japanese defenders knew that hell had descended on them when out of the sky came silver wings pregnant with paratroopers. The paratroopers looked like toys in the sky. Then you could see them pulling on the lines of their chutes, guiding them into the drop zone. Some landed perfectly; others went over the side and onto the mountain to be killed by Japanese hidden there. Some others went into the sea. You could tell when a paratrooper was hit by small-arms fire. He would relax and the chute would take over the landing. One dead paratrooper hung in the white ruins of a destroyed building topside. These brave men were from the 503rd Regimental Combat Team. They did their job and killed the enemy.

Between February 18 and 26, we were engaged in ten shore bombardments and three star shell missions on Corregidor, expending 2700 rounds of 5-inch shells, 70 star shells, and 2500 rounds of 40-mm. Because we were steaming in mined waters, all hands were worried. At Marvellas, both *Lavalette* and *Radford* had hit mines. *Lavalette*, hit in the forward fireroom, suffered 6 dead and 23 wounded. *Radford* had three dead and four wounded. While we were steaming and anchoring in those unswept waters, we were close enough to see the enemy's eyeballs. On a minesweeping operation, our old friends, *Fletcher* and *Hopewell*, came under fire from the "Rock". Six-inch shells hit *Hopewell*; six men died and seven were wounded. *Fletcher* lost six men and had five men wounded. We anchored just off Monkey Point to give fire support and assist in covering for the wounded and dead on landing craft. These craft would tie up at our fantail for help with the critically injured, and then finish the trip to Bataan filled with passengers for the hospital and graveyards.

Two shipmates, W. M. Norman and E. Hillman, told me about the battle close to Monkey Point. Norman recounted, "We were anchored close to Monkey Point in an unswept minefield, about 150 yards from the fighting. Mortars were firing, small-arms fire was at a peak, and our 5-inch shells could not reach the mouth of the cave where the Japanese resistance was greatest. The Army had a tank delivered by an LCVP. It waddled up to the cave. In a few minutes it fired. The whole island shook as big rocks flew into the air and dropped in the sea around the ship. The cave had been an ammunition dump! Everything on Monkey Point was covered by clouds of dust. In a few minutes, individual soldiers started to stand up and move about. I thought all hands had been killed; yet in 15 minutes, things were back to normal with the fight going on like the tank had never existed."

Hillman, who was a welder and steel fabricator, had done an emergency repair job on the drive shaft of the steering engine when we first put to sea. He did such a good job that the repair ship praised the work when we went alongside them for availability. After that, Mr. Rogers, our engineering officer, thought Hillman could do anything. When the Army called for someone to cut the men from the tank caught in the explosion on Monkey Point, Mr. Rogers volunteered Hillman for the job. When Hillman reached the quarterdeck, Rogers was waiting for him with air, gas, 200 feet of hose, and all the tools needed for cutting into the tank. Rogers also gave Hillman his service .45 pistol and helped him strap it on as the cutting outfit was put aboard the Army landing craft. (Hillman didn't know how to shoot the .45, but he didn't say anything.) Upon landing, an Army sergeant was ordered to guard Hillman while they moved to the tank, which was called "Murder, Inc." When they reached the tank, an Army officer told Hillman not to use the torch because the tank was on its back and fuel was spilled all around. Besides, he thought they were all dead. An Army doctor went into the gulley and used a stethoscope on the outside of the tank to listen. When he heard no signs of life, they didn't try to do any more. The doctor had been burned all over his face. Meanwhile, the fighting was still in progress with small-arms fire and mortars. Hillman spied a Japanese rifle, which he reached for, but the sergeant pulled him back, saying it was a booby trap. While Hillman watched, the sergeant found him a clean rifle.

While we were anchored at Monkey Point, an officer who had no rank showing came by with a number of dead and wounded. He only had a shoulder patch saying, "Alamo Scouts." I finally found information on this group of men in a book produced for the 1st Marine Division. Alamo Scouts were called the "Old Breed." Formed by General MacArthur, they were drawn from First and Second Marine Raiders, Solomon Island natives, Australians, Navy underwater demolitions experts, and coast watchers. Quiet killers all, they were used to scout in advance for landing parties. What made me notice this man was the way he sat on a dead man and ate an apple one of our cooks handed to him.

During this time at Monkey Point, a most depressing thing happened, causing me to go back to a time in the Depression. My Dad and I were in Chattahoochee, Florida. We left home early and walked to Cousin Claudia Campbell's house, where I spent the day while Dad looked for work but with no success. On our way back home to River Junction, we saw the police go up to a boy sleeping on a bench near the old Rail Roader's Hotel. One of them placed his club almost on the sleeper's foot and raised it up. When the club hit, the boy came up with a loud yell. Dad knew one of the policemen, a Mr. Dudley, and promised that the boy could stay with us until he could move on. The boy's first name was Buck; I can't remember his last name. He stayed with us for a while and then moved on. He was my age. It made me realize how lucky I was to have a home. My trip back to this time in Florida was caused by an incident at Monkey Point. A landing craft with dead and wounded was tied up to our starboard stern. One of the dead included a paratrooper who had jumped and drifted down the mountainside. He had been trussed to a pole to get him down. His face was so much like Buck's that I was shocked beyond belief. To this day, when my mind takes a walk, it often stops at Monkey Point but returns in a hurry to the present. If by some quirk of fate this body was Buck's, it only helps to prove that death has no dignity and life no purpose.

One of the Japanese hid from the advancing Army patrols behind a rock near the water's edge at Monkey Point. As he was hiding from the soldiers, some of our men shot at him with rifles. He looked at us for a good 30 seconds, armed a grenade, and blew his helmet and his head off in the air. It reminded me of a Japanese song; the last two lines said, "I shall die for the Emperor, I shall never look back."

While we were anchored at Monkey Point, we were hit with fragments of 75-mm shells that landed close aboard, but once again, our mantle of luck was with us. We had been formed as Destroyer Division 46 and given one job to do: Lay the cold hand on the "Rock." We did. The destroyers were all from Desron 22 and 23 of old Guadalcanal days. They were *Converse*, *Thatcher*, *Dyson*, *Claxton*, *Saufley*, and *Cunningham*.

In one day, we destroyed an active 75-mm gun, and we hit caves and pillboxes, a Q-boat, and two barges. On another day, spotters on the beach reported our fire had sealed 20 caves and killed 159 Japanese troops hidden in the caves. At Monkey Point, we could see the whites of the enemies' eyes, we fired for effect, and we could see the job well done without using glasses. As far as I can tell, it was the first time in history a destroyer had anchored so close to active field guns to give fire support and emergency first aid for the U.S. Army. Commander Silk was commended by Commander Destroyer Division 46 for our ship's excellent performance during this operation.

On March 1, 1945, we helped in the invasion of LuBang Islands in the Philippines. On March 10, we were at the invasion of Mindanao; Zamboanga was the town. We were at the invasion of Basilan Island, Philippines, on March 16. Back at Corregidor, we worked through one minefield that was remotely controlled. Right after we went over it, the mine went off. Once again, somebody was looking out for us.

Once at Zamboanga, we were out of meat. The captain had the supply officer tell us he would pay a nickel a pound for all of the fish we caught. We caught enough barracuda to feed the whole ship a couple of meals. I don't know if he ever paid the nickel or not.

Our logistics seemed to be well-planned. The only thing we ever ran out of was food. Ammunition and fuel were always there when we needed it. All we had to do was pull out to the supply ship or the tanker to receive new supplies. In a lull in the action, we pulled alongside an ammunition ship. The merchant seamen didn't want to offload it because it wasn't time for them to start work. Commander Silk sent a boarding party aboard, put them under arrest, and made them load it right away.

By March 1, we were at Tilic Town, Lubang Island, conducting a pre-H-hour bombardment for landing. (H-hour was the hour before the troops were landed.) We were flagship for this set-to. After a four-day availability alongside USS *Dobbin* for food, arms, ammunition, and spare parts, *Saufley* joined the Zamboanga invasion as a screening ship. During this operation, we screened (covered and protected) for the Basilan unit and furnished pre-H-hour bombardment for the Lamitan Town landing force. On March 24, *Saufley* became the flagship for commander of the Sulu Attack Group, with Senior Officers Present Afloat at Zamboanga until the April 21. *Saufley* remained anchored at Zamboanga except for the Sanga Sanga and Jolo missions where she served as screening ship and flagship for the landing on Sanga Sanga.

On the April 2, *Saufley* and several other ships were fired on by Japanese machine guns. We conducted no counterfire because of the close proximity of our own troops. From April 8 until April 11, we were at the Jolo landing and delivered H-hour bombardment.

The next day we silenced a Japanese gun emplacement during a bombardment. When fired on by shore batteries, we always went to high-speed, radical maneuvering (figure eights, zig-zags, circles, and right or left turns). We did anything we could to prevent their getting a fix on us. Since the shore guns were stationary, we always had the advantage and succeeded in silencing the shore batteries most of the time.

From April 22 until May 2, *Saufley* was at Tawitawi Bay, Sulu archipelago, with the Sulu Attack Group in charge of the minesweeping operations. When mines were cut loose from their moorings, they surfaced and became floating mines. We had sharpshooters stationed all over the ship to spot and shoot at these deadly devils. With help from the 40-mm and 20-mm guns, we usually destroyed them very quickly. If a mine came to the surface close to us, all we could do was "cut thin washers" and hope we didn't bump it. At these times, those of us below decks always got nervous.

After Sulu, *Saufley* operated near the Morotai, Halmahera Group, escorting convoys between Morotai and Leyte. About this time, I was down in the ice machine room and saw that the officers' mess boys had set out a round cardboard carton of raspberries to thaw. I grabbed the berries and headed for the engine room with O. R. Elliott following me and using a rag to wipe up the spilled juice as we ran down the deck. We called all the off-duty engine room crew and, in less than 30 minutes, all the berries were gone. As punishment, Commander Silk came on the loudspeaker and announced that he was taking away our bread ration for three days. He offered to give it back if anyone would identify the thieves. No one did, and we still got our bread. Everyone was happy to know that at least the gang in the forward engine room had berries to eat.

On April 28, Benito Mussolini died. All the Italian sailors were overjoyed with this news and talked about it for several days. After being tried and shot, Mussolini was hung head down for the people to see. He had cried, "Let me live, let me live, and I will give you an Empire." He got off easy as far as I was concerned! Two days later, April 30, Adolf Hitler was dead by his own hand. How sad! I wish the Russians had captured him and delivered him to the survivors of Stalingrad as their pet. I'm sure they would have fixed him for good. Every man aboard was happy about Hitler's death; he had been hated all over the earth.

From May 21 until May 28, we were alongside USS *Whitney* for structural repairs because nearby explosions had bent our hull. On June 3, *Saufley* left Morotai with a convoy to Brunci Bay, British North Borneo, the only time we were involved with British ground troops. It reminded me of the seemingly long-ago time at Scapa Flow. Everything went as planned on this all-British landing. *Saufley* screened the unloading operation and reported to the Miri-Lutong area to cover minesweeping operations there. Three days later, we departed for Morotai.

On June 26, *Saufley* left with the invasion force for Balik-papan, serving as screening and bombardment ship. On this operation, we fired 1000 rounds of 5-inch shells, knocking out many coastal defense guns and machine guns and destroying many troops as well. As we were approaching Balikpapan, we could see black smoke from burning oil tanks and supply dumps. For the 20 or more days we were in this area, the pall of smoke hung over the port and the outskirts of the city. When the wind shifted to sea, you could taste burnt oil in the air. I have never seen another fire to equal this one. After completing this operation, *Saufley* reported to the Leyte area until August 5, when we left for Ulithi, Caroline Islands, to Commander Marianas Group for escort duty because of the submarine threat in this area.

About this time, everyone began to realize we had won, but we knew that many of us were yet to die in the process of finishing off the Japanese home islands. The Japanese suicide missions had sunk many of our sister ships; many of our men had been killed or wounded. Destroyers were still judged to be the first line of defense against these missions. These were not pleasant thoughts for a man to live with.

Just before our realization of victory, cruiser *Indianapolis* was sunk between Saipan and Leyte Gulf with the bulk of her crew lost. She had just delivered the first atom bomb to *Enola Gay* for deposit in Japan. When we received the news of the dropping of the first atom bomb and the death and destruction it had wrought, we all believed that Navy scuttlebutt had almost been on target with rumors of a bomb that would end the war. We didn't know then what it was made of, but by the time the second bomb hit, we were all discussing how to split atoms even though we didn't understand the effects of an atomic explosion. We even had long, uninformed talks about Einstein's theory. No one could really understand the evil the atom bomb had unleashed. Then, when the Japanese still refused to surrender, we took a long look at the future. We knew that many more of us would die and the result would still be the same: We must win.

Our last week of the war was spent escorting ships between Ulithi and Leyte. The first atom bomb hit Hiroshima August 6, 1945, and for all practical purposes, the war was over. The propaganda coming out of Japan still focused on a fight to the finish. On August 9, a second bomb hit Nagasaki, which was eradicated, but the Japanese leaders still wouldn't surrender. Then, Russia belatedly declared war on Japan, and our vast fleet continued to pound them everywhere. Carrier planes and B29s from Saipan and Tinian bombed Japan every day.

At this time, everywhere the Japanese forces stood, they were in mortal danger. Their once mighty fleet was gone. Using Japanese figures, we figured that they had lost 11 battleships, 21 aircraft carriers, 38 cruisers, 135 destroyers, and 134 submarines. The Japanese military officers who caused the war were still in control; the Emperor was the only one who could put an end to the rule by the military over the Japanese. He finally issued an Imperial order to stop the war.

The war was over. On August 14, 1945, the cease-fire was flashed to the fleet. The surrender of the Japanese was a real surprise to all of us who had fought them for so long. We did not trust them to do anything except fight to the very last man. Suddenly it was over. All the old hands were shocked. We had thought for years of the invasion of Japan, had looked forward to it, and at the same time, knew our luck was sure to run out at some future battle site. Even though the peace was won, we couldn't adjust to lights at night, or days and nights free from General Quarters. No one was trying to kill us, but it was hard to adjust to peace. The newer sailors were happy and sad at the same time. The veterans had the battle stars and discharge points, and we were leaving for the States on every available ship. The best sailors in the world were going home. Our enlistment was up and by law we had to be sent home.

What would I do? Go back to school? Get in the Merchant Marine? Farm? Get married? Stay in the Navy? Everything was up in the air and, for the first time since I joined the Navy, I was worried about what to do. I had only known the Great Depression, death, and destruction. I had never had a civilian job; I had never even had a special girl friend. I was frightened. I was 22 years old and had been in the Navy since I was 17. I didn't know how to be a civilian.

We were anchored in Leyte Gulf in August 1945, and the war was over. On August 14, Emory Joseph Jernigan, with his seabag already packed for days, was on his way home together with A. C. Newby, J. R. Barry, C. W. Deal, Red Robertson, W. T. Harland, and a few more whose names I can't remember. Newby and I said a sad goodby to Fagan; he was our brother forever. *Saufley* had been my home for over three years while we fought the Japanese. I had earned 16 battle stars on that ship. As we left, I stared at her there dead in the water. It was the first time I had seen her without a set defense since we put to sea. I started to yell out, "Wait, that's not right," but it was over.

EPILOGUE

In early September, Saufley *moved up to the Ryukyus and then proceeded to the China coast. She assisted in minesweeping operations in the Yangtze delta area. The destroyer remained off the coast of China until she departed for home on 12 November. Arriving at San Diego at the end of the year,* Saufley *continued on to the east coast in mid-January 1946. During February, she underwent repairs at the New York Naval Shipyard. In early March,* Saufley *headed south to Charleston for inactivation.*

Decommissioned on 12 June 1946, Saufley *remained in the Reserve Fleet for just over three years. Redesignated DDE-465 on 15 March 1949, she was recommissioned on 15 December 1949 and assigned to Escort Destroyer Squadron (CortDesRon) 2, Atlantic Fleet. Within a year, she had participated in two search and rescue operations. The first, in June 1950, was the rescue of 36 passengers from a downed commercial airliner on a Puerto Rico-New York run. The second, in October, was the rescue of a Navy TBM pilot assigned to* Palau *(CVA-122).*

On 1 January 1951, the escort destroyer was reclassified an Experimental Escort Destroyer, EDDE-465, and assigned to experimental work under the control of Commander, Operational Development Force. A unit of DesDiv 601, she was home ported at Key West; and, for the next twelve years, was primarily engaged in testing and evaluating sonar equipment and antisubmarine warfare weapons.

On 1 July 1962, Saufley *was redesignated a general purpose destroyer and regained her original designation, DD-465. At the end of that month, she participated in the filming of the movie "PT-109". In September, she resumed test and evaluation work. In late October, she was placed on standby; and, after, the proclamation of the Cuban Quarantine, she commenced patrols off the coast of Florida. She con-*

*tinued that duty until 20 November, then returned to Key West. On the
26th, she participated in a Presidential review of the Quarantine
Force.*

For the next two years, Saufley *continued her experimental projects, interrupting those operations only for scheduled exercises, sonar
school ship duties; and, in the spring of 1963, assistance in the search
for* Thresher *(SSN-563).*

Ordered back to Norfolk in the fall of 1964, Saufley *was decommissioned on 29 January 1965. Her use as an experimental ship,
however, continued. In 1967, instruments and gauges to register strain
and stress of successive explosions were installed; and, in February
1968, as a result of tests, she was sunk off Key West.*

Saufley *earned 16 battle stars during World War II.*

—from The Dictionary of American Naval Fighting Ships

We arrived at Cavite Navy Base and were put in tents situated
in a drainage ditch. The rainwater came through the tents two
or three times a day. We learned about graft, pooled our
resources, and bribed the ship assignment yeoman with a new
radio. The next day, we boarded the troopship *General R. M.
Blatchford* and headed home by way of Ulithi anchorage. I
volunteered to stand watches in exchange for crew privileges.
At Ulithi, we went on a liberty party led by a Catholic priest.
When they went to get beer, I joined the working party in the
storage room. I worked on my shoestrings until I was the last
one to get my case of beer. They turned right, I turned left,
and the rest is history. The priest was a good guy and never
said anything.

After Ulithi, we headed for Seattle on the northern route,
which was very cold. The cold weather caused all of us who
had spent time in the tropics to go to the bathroom at least
once an hour day and night. It seemed that the body's cooling
system retained water longer in a hot climate, and sweating
caused one to drink more.

We arrived in Seattle, Washington, and were assigned to
bunks in the naval station. I got drunk every day and missed
the troop trains for over a week. A chief I had known before

put me on restriction and saw that I boarded my troop train the next day. I was routed through Arkansas, Atlanta, and finally into Jacksonville. When I arrived in Jacksonville for discharge, soldiers of the Afrika Korps were serving chow on the chow line. They were all small, blond, and blue-eyed; I wanted to drag one across the chow line, but my longing to get out caused me to back off.

I was discharged October 16, 1945, went home, and played around. On October 19, I met Ann Rivenbark, and that was the end of my free life. I became her slave. We were married November 25, 1945, and had three children. We also have six grandchildren and one great-grandchild. On October 31, 1989, at 3:45 AM, Ann Rivenbark Jernigan, my dear wife of 44 years crossed the bar. Life on this earth will never be the same for me.

Let me tell you in closing what happened to some of the significant people in my Navy career. Jim Fagan, my friend for many years, died. I was present for his funeral when his wife, Mary, received a call from Captain Brown who said Jim was a good shipmate. Mary cried and said it was like a call from God. She told all her family and grandchildren right away. May the good Lord hold him close. We loved each other.

Captain Cochran, who was a very humane man, started getting nervous at the suicide cliffs. The civilian deaths hurt him more than any of us. He left the ship after the suicide missions in the Philippines and retired to California where he died. His ashes were scattered at sea. This writer truly believes Captain Cochran did more to bring us home safely than anyone else.

Captain Brown made rear admiral and retired to Washington, D.C., where he lived in the shadow of his beloved Mormon Temple. When he died, one of our shipmates represented *Saufley* at his funeral in Arlington Cemetery.

Finally, I'd like to say some special words about what the word, shipmate, means to me. Shipmate is an honorable word that is earned, not given. Being called a shipmate is the highest compliment one can earn in this life. Shipmate is a word equal to none in the English language. It is filled with courage, love, hate, duty, honor, and country. It is a bond forged in storms, battles, adversity, and victory, and it is equaled only by a man's love for his wife and family. It is formed at sea in a ship with a captain of character who causes a "can-do" spirit to pass down the line: captain to executive officer to junior officers, chiefs, petty officers, and crew. Weak links are cut loose and replaced quickly and cleanly without fanfare by a wise captain. We were lucky with Commander Brown. Everything happened like a well-written script, that is, the good ship, the good crew, and a bonding forged so strong it can be broken only by the death of the last shipmate. This bond, this ship, and our great good luck are the reasons we survived and won.

INDEX

Aaron Ward, USS, 153
Aberdeen Proving Grounds, 82
Addison, Donald, 110
Afrika Korps, 197
Alamo Scouts, 187
Alarid, Alfonso B., 177
Allen, Evan, 177
Allen, Raymond W., 177
Anzio beachhead, 168
Aqua Velva, 26
Arab's Tent, 28
Arctic Circle, 33, 89
Arizona Memorial, 156
Arkansas, 197
Arlington Cemetery, 195
Asiatic fleet, 81, 89, 110, 134
Atlanta, GA, 197
Atlantic Ocean, 43, 171
atom bomb, 192
Aulick USS, 177
Australia, 47, 128, 187
Australian Divisions 7 & 9, 133, 148

Bailey, Lewis F., 177
Balboa, 89
Balikpapan, Borneo, 175, 191
ball and chain emblem, 154
Baltimore, 31
Bangert, John C., 89, 142
Banika Islands, 94
Barry, J. R., 193
Barton, USS, 153
Basilan Island, 189
Bataan, 184, 186
Baum, Charlie, 154
Bay Bridge, 164, 166
Ben Milam Hotel, 166
Benham, USS, 153
Benson, Admiral William S., 37
Benson, Captain H. H. J., 37, 60
Berry, J. R. 126, 129, 133
Bethlehem Steel Yard, 163, 165
Bismark, 61

Black Gang, 32
Blackett Straight, 105, 167
Bligh, Captain, 184
Blighty, 53
Blue, USS, 153
Blue Jacket's Manual, 21
Bofors, 82
Borneo, Balikpapan, 175
Bougainville, 95, 105, 106, 146, 150, 167
Bounty, 184
Boyes, Lieutenant John L., 165, 177
Brinkman, B. J., 131
British Home Fleet, 58, 60
Brooklyn Navy Yard, 50, 77, 80, 178
Brooklyn, NY, 50
Broom, Doris, 27
Brown, Commander Bert, 77, 78, 81, 99, 100, 109, 118, 124, 125, 131 140, 147, 154, 183, 197, 198
Brownsen, USS, 153
Brunci Bay, 191
Buka, 105
Burger, Herman, 164
Burke, Commodore 99, 100, 168
burial at sea, 141
Burma Shave, 16

Caballo, 184
Cade, H. A., 42, 44, 56, 71
Calebra, 88
Camotes Sea, 174
Camp 1410, 14
Campbell, Claudia 187
Canada, 14
canal zone, 90
Cape Esperance, 94, 105
Cape St. George, 105, 150, 167
captain of the head, 23, 131
captain's barge, 41
Captain's Mast, 37
Caroline Islands, 191
Casco Bay, MA 42, 57, 81

catfever, 23
Cavite Navy Base, 196
Central Park, NY, 50
Charleston, SC, 195
Chattahoochee, FL 13, 27, 166, 187
Chevalier, USS, 153
China, 52, 92
Choiseul, 138, 167
Christmas 23, 96-97, 108, 130, 148, 150
Christmas Eve, 23, 34, 37-39, 43
Civilian Conservation Corp, 13
Clarke, W.P.O., 39
Claxton USS, 188
Clearwater, FL, 109
Cochran, Dale Eugene, 77, 81, 82, 86, 99, 116, 131, 137, 140, 147, 148, 154, 156, 164, 169, 178, 183, 197
Colleran, Chief, 140
Colombus, USS, 88, 109
Colon, 88
Colsens 64
cooks, 91, 92
Cooper USS, 180
Commander Destroyer Division 46, 188
Commander Marianas Group, 191
Commander Silk, 116, 183, 184
Commander South Pacific, 92
Commodore Burke, 99, 100
Coney Island, 50
Converse, USS 188
Cony, USS 143
Corregidor, 82, 116, 184, 185, 189
Cotter, Red, 124
Cromie, 108
Cumberland, HMS 72
Cuba, Guantanamo Bay, 42
Cuban quarantine, 195
Cunningham USS, 188
Curley, Chief, 108, 110, 144
Cushing, USS, 153
Cyr, Art, 124, 177
Czechowski, Eddie, 150, 151

Daloia, Frank T., 177

Dare, George W., 177
Deal, C. W., 193
Deal, "Skinhead," 150
Deer, Pappy, 126
DeGuiseppe, 126
DeHaven, USS, 88, 97, 153
Dempsey, Jack, 31
Denton, L. L., 33, 42, 56
DeRosa, Paul, 100, 130
DeSimone, Nick, 155
Desron Eight
Desron Twenty-Two
Desron Twenty-Three
Destroyer Division 46, 188
Destroyer Division 122, 147
Destroyer Squadron Twenty-Two, 124, 144, 154
Devine, Joseph F., 177
Dewey, Admiral, 38
Diamond Head, 156, 163
DiBenedetto, James A., 177
Dittimore, 38
77th Division, 180
Dobbin, USS, 99, 189
Dolans, 64
Donato, Maury G., 177
Dougher, Albert I., 177
Doughty, 143
Dowling, Joe, 124
Dudley, Mr., 187
Duffy, George, 108, 130, 165, 184
Duke of York HMS, 61, 72
Duncan, USS, 153
Duprey, James 143, 177
Dyson USS, 188

Eabon, Tony, 140, 143, 177, 183
East Coast, 88
Echo HMS, 61
Eckel, 173
Eddie Hotel, 168
Eddy, Mary Baker, 165
Edinburg, 60
Edsall, USS, 153
Edwards, Frank S., 137
Einhorn, Rudolph, 84, 130
Einsten, 192

Elliott, Ray, 84, 117, 130, 133, 170, 190
Ellis, Frank, 167
Ellyson, USS 58
Ely, C. E., 14
Emeru Island, 146, 151
Empress Augusta Bay, 95, 105, 125, 151, 157
Englehardt, 130, 177
Enola Gay, 192
Escort Destroyer Squadron, 195
Espirito Santo, 95, 96, 138

Fagan, Jim, 108, 109, 112, 113, 124, 126, 129, 133, 147, 156, 169, 170, 193, 197
feather merchants, 52
Federal Shipbuilding and Dry Dock Co., 77
Federal Shipbuilding Yard, 80
Fisherman's Wharf, 169
Filipino, 37
Fletcher, 185
Fletcher-class destroyers, 97, 153
Ford Island, 156
Foss, Major Joe, 116, 150
Fox, 38
Franks USS, 156
French, 92
Fry, Charlie, 34
Fujisawa, Lt. Cmr., 125

Gaillard, 88
galley slaves, 41
General Electric, 32, 178
General R. M. Blatchford, USNS, 196
Geneva Convention, 159
Giffen, Rear Admiral, 60
Goodlett, 113
Grand Canyon, 36
Grapan Town, 158, 159
Gravesend Bay, 42
Great Depression, 193
Green Island, 105, 146, 150
Greer, USS, 53

Guadalcanal, 77, 92, 94-105, 118, 119, 145, 188
Guam, 146, 160
Guantanamo Bay, 42
Gulledge, Walter L., 98
Gwin, USS, 153

Haiti, 42
Halmahera Group, 190
Halsey, Admiral, 95, 100, 109, 118, 119
Hamilton, L.H.K., 72
Harland, W. T., 193
Hastings, Chief, 139, 144, 175
Hastings, Don, 177
Havana Harbor, 99
Helena (USS), 167
Helminiak, Clement, 117
Henderson Field, 105
Henley, USS, 153
Hillman, E., 186, 187
Hipper, 60
Hiroshima, 192
Hitler, 53, 190, 191
Hollandia, New Guinea, 181
Hopewell, 185
Horn, Edward N., 177
Hornet, USS 57
Houston, TX 80, 166
Huffine, Dr. C.R., 113, 144, 145, 163
Huffine, N. H., 131
Huie, D. R., 136, 137
Hunter's Point, 32, 165

I-2, 146
Iceland, Reykjavik, 62, 70
Idaho USS, 57
Indianapolis, USS, 137, 191
Indispensable Straight, 95
Ingram, USCG, 183
Irisher Club, 168, 169
Ironbottom Sound, 95, 105, 167

Jacksonville, FL, 14, 15, 197
Japanese army forces, 52

Japanese suicide planes, 181, 182,
    191
Jarvis, USS, 153
Jenkintown, 34
Jernigan, Ferrell, 13
Jernigan, James, 13
Jernigan, Mattie, 13
Jernigan, Mattie Lee, 13
Jernigan, Naomi, 13
Jernigan, Thomas, 13
John Penn SS, 104
Johnson, Lt. W. R., 15
Johnson City, TN 131
Jolo mission, 189
Jones, Casey, 157
Jones, Dr., 133, 151
Jones, Robert E. Lee, 176, 177
Jutland, Battle of 56

"k" guns, 82
kamikazes, 181
Kearney, NJ, 80
Kearney USS, 53
Kennedy, John F., 142
Keppell HMS, 72
Key West, 196
kiddie cruise, 15
King George, 65
King George V, HMS 61, 69, 70
kingfisher, 43
Kipling, Rudyard, 101
Klingensmith, John C., 166
Knight, Jim, 78, 109, 119, 163, 165,
    170
Knox, Frank, 39
Kokumbona, 97
Kolombangara, 105, 138
Kondo, Lt. Cmdr. Fumitake, 175
Krieger, Boatswain, 147, 169, 172
Kula Gulf, 167
Kwajalein, 156

Laffey, USS, 153
Lake Gatun, 88
Lamitan Town, 189
Lang, USS 58, 61
Larned, John J., 124, 150

Larson, Art, 150
Lavalette, 185
LCI's, 139
LeBlanc, William E., 91
Lee, Ernest F., 177
Levinson, Alan, 106, 109, 110, 118
Leyte Gulf, 174, 175, 183, 190, 191,
    192, 193
Liberty Bell, 50
liberty hog, 49
Life magazine, 112
Lingayan Gulf, 98, 174, 181, 182,
    183
Little, J. P., 70
Livermore USS, 57
London HMS, 72
Long Island, USS, 57
Look magazine, 112
LST 396, 140
LuBang Islands, 188, 189
Lunga Point, Guadalcanal, 92, 94,
    105, 118
Lützow, 60
Luzon Island, 174, 182
Lyon, Lloyd L., 177

MacArthur, General, 175, 187
Macon, GA, 14
Madison, USS, 58, 61
Manila Bay, 174
Manus Island, 180
Marianas, 146, 160, 163
Marines, 14, 28, 52, 89, 117, 129,
    157, 158, 159
Maripa Point, 159
Marne, HMS 69
Marshall, Lieut., 124
Martin, USS, 69
Martin, Glen W., 14
Martin, W. J., Lieutenant, 142, 157
Marvellas, 184, 185
Maryland, 82
Maryland (USS), 180
Massachusetts, USS, 37
Matheson, Captain R. W., 31
McAdams, Chief, 108
McAlpin, 64, 101

McCullough, G. H., 177
McVey, Capt., 137
Meadows, John Thomas, 52
Meredith, USS, 153
Mettick, Chief 17-21
Michie, Dan, 165, 166
Mid-City Club, 35
Military Cemetery, Guadalcanal, 144
Miller, R. I., 74
Mindanao, 188
Mindoro, 174, 183
Minneapolis (USS), 95, 96
Miri-Lutong, 191
Mississippi, USS, 57
Mondeair, Chief, 44, 56, 62, 71, 80
Monkey Point, 82, 186, 187, 188
Monssen, USS, 153
Montgomery (USS), 138
Mormon Temple, 195
Morotai, 174, 183, 190, 191
Mote, A. N., 112
mount captain, 82
Mowrey, Pop, 100
Munda, 105
"Murder, Inc.", 186
Murmansk-Archangel, 77
Mussolini, Benito, 190

Nagasaki, 192
Namatanai Air Field, 150
Nasugbu landing, 174, 177, 183
Navy
  base, 14, 16
  craft, 158
  dependant allotment, 29
  fliers, 80
  pre-war, 155
  reserves, 52
  two-ocean, 153
  underwater demolitions experts, 187
  yard, 164
Naval Academy, 80
Naval operating base, 16, 27, 27, 30-31, 42
Naval support facilities, 28

New Caledonia, 92, 97, 105, 145
New England, 77
New Georgia, 105, 144, 127
New Guinea, 181
New Hebrides, 95, 99, 105, 127
New Mexico USS, 57
New Orleans, LA 166
New York City, 80, 134
New York Times, 47, 108
New York USS, 57
New York Naval shipyard, 195
Newby, A. C., 113, 126, 169, 170, 193
Newport News, VA, 28
Newsweek, 112
Nicholas, USS, 97
Nigeria, HMS, 72
Norfolk HMS, 72
Norfolk, VA, 54, 56, 57, 77, 88
Norman, Willis Martin, 112, 119, 126, 186
North Atlantic, 42, 88
North Carolina, 88, 122
Noumea, New Caledonia, 77, 105

Oakland, CA 168
O'Brien, USS, 153
Octogen Soap Company, 20
Oerlikon, 82
Officer's Country, 37
oil king, 156
Okinawa, 147
Olympia, USS, 38-39
Operation "Cleanslate," 94
Operation Forager, 146
O'Reilly, 126, 129
Ormoc Bay, 175, 180
Owen, Howard, 124

P38 Lightnings, 106
Pacific Ocean, 43, 81, 89, 90, 170
Pacific War, 117, 151
Panama, 88
Panama Canal, 88
Parker, Andy L., 177
Parris Island, SC, 24
Pavuvu, 94

Pearl Harbor, 54-55, 80, 89, 92,
    146, 155, 156, 163, 184
Pensacola, 80
Pennsylvania USS, 54
Perkins, USS, 153
Phifer, Tom C., 81, 86, 91
Philadelphia, PA, 31, 34, 49
Philadelphia Navy Yard, 35
Philippines, 98, 137, 180, 188, 197
Phillips, USS, 143
Phipps, Lloyd C., 177
Pilar Point, 174
Pizzo, Anthony B., 177
Plunkett USS, 57
pom-pom guns, 36
Ponson Island, 174
Port-au-Prince, Haiti, 50
Portland, MA, 58
Porter, USS, 153
Portsmouth, VA 27
Portsmouth Naval Hospital, 26
PQ17, 89
Preston, USS, 153
Prince of Wales HMS, 66
Pringle, USS, 177
PT 109, 142, 196
Punjabi, HMS, 69, 70
Purvis Bay, 105

Rabaul, 95, 105, 119, 146, 148, 150,
    151
Radford, USS, 185
Rail Roader's Hotel, 187
Ranger, USS, 17
Reader's Digest, 112
Reagan, Ronald, 153
Red Cross, 168
503 Regimental Combat Team, 185
Rendova, 94, 105
Reno, USS, 176
Renshaw USS, 143, 174, 175
Repulse HMS, 66
Reuben James USS, 53
Reykjavik, Iceland 62, 70
Rigel, USS, 99
Rivenbark, Ann 195
River Junction, 167, 187

RO-101, 138
Road To Mandalay, 101
Robertson, Red 193
Rodney, 65
Rogers, J. W., 86, 186
Rogers, Lt., 108, 112
Rogers, Wynt, 108, 152
Romero, Caesar, 153
Roosevelt
Eleanor, 118
Franklin D., 13
Rosebud, TX, 84
Ross, Lieutenant J. G., 39, 57, 80
Rossiter, Keith, 122
Rowan USS, 72
"Royal Baby's Butt," 91
Royal Oak, HMS, 60
Ruddock, T.D., Admiral, 180
Russell Island, 94, 98, 105
Russia, 192
Ryukyus, 195

Saddler, 124
Saipan, 137, 146, 156, 158, 159,
    160, 159, 160, 181, 191
salvo, 48
Samuels, Mickey, 106
San Cristobal, 105
San Diego, 155, 170, 196
San Francisco, 126, 155, 163, 164,
    166, 167, 168, 184
Sand Street, 50, 78, 109
Sanga Sanga, 174, 189
Saturday Evening Post, 112
Saufley
Field, 80
Helen, 80
Lieutenant (jg) Richard Coswell,
    80
Savo, 94, 95, 105, 148, 167
Scapa Flow, Scotland, 56, 58, 60,
    64, 65, 66, 191
Scheer, Admiral, 60
Scruggs, Mrs. Helen O. R., 77
Sea Lark Channell, 105
"Sea Pappy," 84
Seabees, 139, 159

Seattle, 196
Secretary of the Navy, 39
Shamrock Beer Garden, 27
shanker mechanics, 52
Shaw, 126
Shore Patrol, 49
Shortland Island, 105
Silk, Commander F. W., 116, 183, 184, 189
Simms, USS, 153
"Slot", the, 105, 110, 116, 118, 119, 123, 124, 125, 142, 148
Smith, 116
Smith, Douglas R., 177
Solomons, 82, 105, 119, 125, 132, 138, 148, 151-155, 175, 187
Somali, HMS 72
South Atlantic, 43, 47
South Pacific, 77, 89, 92, 104, 147
Southern Cross, 101, 105
Spam, 92, 127, 128, 144, 168
Stalingrad, 191
Stoneham, George Abner, 84, 109, 126
Strong, USS, 153
submarine, 138, 141, 146, 151, 156
Subic Bay, 174, 183
Suicide Cliffs, Saipan, 159
Sullivan brothers, 95
Sulu Archipelago, 190
Sulu Attack group, 189, 190
Sulu Sea, 174
Swan, Robert H., 119, 126, 177
Swanson, Mr., 178
Sydney, Australia, 47, 99-101, 105, 128, 132-134, 147, 148

Tannenbaum, Joe, 106
Task Force 11, 94
Task Force 51, 18, 146
Task Force 67, 95, 96
Tassafaronga, 94, 105
tatoo artists, 28
Tawitawi Bay, 190
Tenura River, 105
Tennessee, 131

Texas, 80
Thatcher 188
Thompson, 19
Thompson, E. T., 134
Thompson, Chief R. H., 155
Tilic Town, LuBang Island, 189
Time, 112
Tinian, 147, 157, 160, 162, 192
Tirpitz, 60, 69
Tokyo, 162
"Tokyo Express," 118, 124, 143
Tovey, Sir John, 61
Treasury Islands, 105
Tucker, USS, 153
Tulagi, 95, 105, 106, 109, 118, 136, 141, 142, 152
Tunney, Gene, 31
Tuscaloosa USS, 58, 72

U-boats, 53
Ulithi, 137, 160, 174, 175, 178, 191, 192, 196
Uribi HMS, 69

Val, 181, 182
Vella Gulf, 105, 167
Vella Lavella, 105, 127, 138, 139, 140
Victorious, HMS, 72
Vietnam War, 184

Wainwright, USS, 61, 72
Walke, USS, 153
Walking the floor over you, 28
Waller, USS, 174, 175
Walsh, Lieutenant, 39
Washington, USS, 31-76, 78, 80, 89, 178
Washington, DC, 195
Wasp USS, 57, 60
Watts, Carl, 122, 177
Wayne, John, 153
Westinghouse, 32
Wexelblatt, 14
whiskey ship, 100
Whitney USS, 128, 191

Wichita USS, 57, 60, 72
Wilcox, J. W., Rear Admiral, 57,
    58, 60, 171
Wilhelm, Frederick, 100
Williams, Esther, 112
Wilson USS, 58, 61
Wilson, James H., 177
wonders, 90 day, 52
Wood, Wyatt B., 144, 163
World War I, 16, 82, 53, 56
World War II, 52, 196

Wright, Harry, 129

Yamaguchi, Kazuo, 151
Yamamoto, Admiral, 106
Yangtze Delta, 196

Zamboanga, 188, 189
Zeilin, USS 183
Zero, 158
Zivic, Fritzie, 109